Wealth for Women: Conversations with the Team that Creates the Dream

The Top Female Professionals Who Can Help You Get Wealthy in Real Estate

Chimene Van Gundy and other Investment Professionals

FEATURING

Monick Paul Halm; Caeli Ridge; Laure Marmontel;
Lanisha Stubbs; Marijo Wilson, Ph.D.; Linda Liberatore;
Daniella Dhillon; Lydia Monroy; Zabrina Horton; Felecia Froe, MD;
Deba Harper; Justine Gonzalez; Marie Grasmeier; Michelle Bosch;
Kimle Nailer; Paige Panzarello; Carolyn 'CJ' Matthews

Publishing Company: Smart Hustle Agency & Publishing, LP
www.smarthustleagency.com

Copyright © 2018 Smart Hustle Agency & Publishing, LP

Published by Smart Hustle Agency & Publishing, LP, Los Angeles, CA

The Publisher has strived to be as accurate and complete as possible in the creation of this book. This book is not intended for use as a source of legal, business, accounting, or financial advice. All readers are advised to seek the services of competent professionals in legal, business, accounting, medical, and financial fields. In practical advice books, like anything else in life, there are no guarantees of income made. Readers are cautioned to rely on their own judgment about their individual circumstances and to act accordingly.

Title: Wealth for Women

Sub Title: Conversations with the Team that Creates the Dream – The Top Female Professionals Who Can Help You Get Wealthy in Real Estate – Chimene Van Gundy and other Investment Professionals

ISBN-13: 9781731531582

Royalties from the Retail Sales of Wealth for Women are donated to TOFi™ Foundation, Inc.

TOFi™ Foundation, Inc. 501(c)3 is a nonprofit organization

TOFi™ Foundation, Inc. is the philanthropic endeavor of Tamla Oates-Forney, who is dedicated to empowering women and girls of color. The mission of TOFi™ Foundation, Inc., is to transform the world by investing in a woman or girl (of color). TOFi™ Foundation, Inc., is focused on developing initiatives to support the needs of women and girls of color through all walks of life—from cradle to CEO, including education, mentorships, personal and professional development, entrepreneurial training, and health and wellness programming. For more information, visitwww.tofifoundation.org/

Scan this QR code to learn more about *A Message in a Bottle* book projects:

Acknowledgments

I would like to acknowledge my VIPs. The list of people who helped deliver my twins, the *Wealth for Women* book and the new book series *A Message in a Bottle*, include but is not limited to: Tera Jenkins, project manager; Isaac Antenyi, editor; Candace Howze, editor; Cristina Salinas, publicist; Nik Boskovski, graphic designer; Kynia Starkey, social media graphic designer. To Heather Mize & Tera Jenkins, both of you have been a net at the bottom of the mountain; to Benjamin Marcus, who came in like a knight in shining armour and brought us to the finish line; and to countless others whose contribution made a difference.

I am grateful to each contributing author—for your patience, understanding and kindness through the conception, gestation, and birthing process of this book and for heart to give back and be a part of something bigger than yourselves.

Finally, I can't express enough gratitude to my family & friends. An acknowledgment to my children, my daughter Aniya Williams for her endless encouragement and faith in me and to my son Daniel Williams: both of you keep me pressing toward the mark. To my sister Andrea Steward for all the support you've given me along the way and making sure that I was eating; to Tamika Bridgewater, my silent partner and prayer warrior; and to my mother, Dolores Steward. Thank you, mommy, for being my rock.

And last but absolutely not least, to my business partner, my father, my provider, my healer—Jesus Christ.

–Lisa Charlene Williams

Foreword

When I was pregnant with my daughter and started having labor pains, we went to the hospital, and the doctor sent us back home. Several hours later, we went back to the hospital because the labor pains were worse and closer. If you've ever been pregnant and experienced labor pains, you know that they can make you want to quit, give up, or of course, kill someone! I was so tired when we returned to the hospital; I told my family, "You know what, guys? I'm tired, and she's not coming, so let's just go back home."

I have learned that birthing a vision, birthing a book series, and birthing a book is very much like being pregnant and delivering a baby. Some pregnancies are a breeze, nine months in and out—beautiful baby. Another pregnancy, there can be horrible morning sickness, your body hurts, and labor pains make you want to climb a wall—and, God forbid, complications during delivery. So, evidentially, any birthing process is a process that can make you want to quit. Like a pregnancy, no matter how much pain or discomfort you may have experienced, no matter how hard and close the labor pains were that made you feel like you couldn't take anymore, once you birthed your child and the doctor put your baby in your arms, all the stress and pain dissolved. And so it is with a vision, a book series, and a book. When you are birthing someone or something that can impact and change the lives of people, there can be warfare and resistance to make you want to turn back, throw in the towel, or quit.

This book project has come to pass in one of the most challenging junctures in my life, so I am confident that there is much purpose attached to it. So, to all the readers who receive a copy of this book either by gift or purchase, young and old, financially secure or trying to get your footing. My prayer is that this book reaches you and something that is shared opens your eyes to possibilities, ignites a fire in your heart, or becomes a resource that lights the pathway to a dream that has been on the shelf. Lastly, I pray this book reaches you as if you were sitting on a deserted island, and a bottle washes up to shore with the very message and information you need at this juncture in your life and impacts your life and your generations to come. And if so, then all the sacrifice and labor pains will have been worth it.

And finally ... my heart's desire is for millions of copies of the *A Message in a Bottle* book to be purchased by the contributors and sponsors so books can be given and gifted to the intended audiences. And also, that the contributors and the nonprofits attached to the books will receive increased visibility and growth that turns into relationships, clients, and revenue.

May the desires of my heart align with God's will.

Do not be anxious about anything, but in every situation, by prayer and petition, with thanksgiving, present your requests to God.
–Philippians 4:6

Table of Contents

A Smarter Hustle That Affords You Lifestyle Independence

Being a modern woman in today's world is complicated. No one needs to tell us how difficult it is to be a female in our constantly changing culture. Whether you are a CEO with a seat at the table, a stay-at-home wife and mother, a single mom working outside the home while raising your children, or a millennial who just graduated from college—entering today's working world—we are ALL busy, busy, busy.

No matter what stage of life you are at, family, friends, children, finding time to date and work responsibilities seem to always be vying for the precious commodity called time. We are told that we can have it all, and so we run ourselves ragged, literally running hither, thither and yon, trying to keep all of our plates spinning in the quest for the American dream of financial security and job success, all while desperately trying to maintain our health and happiness. This is a tough job for even the strongest of women. Our plates are not only spinning; they are full!

And we are out there creating side hustles, grinding, making moves and making things happen for ourselves. But ladies, many of us could be on the verge of working ourselves to death! There is a smarter hustle and a smarter grind. Women are diagnosed with and die from disease more than any other reason—heart disease, cancer, stroke, diabetes—many of these caused by overwork and stress. You have to strategically manage your balls in the air, and the most effective way to do that is to have multiple and passive streams of income coming in. So, God forbid, if you got sick, wanted to take a leave of absence, weren't able to oversee your business, or got yourself buried in student loan debt, you will have the financial means and security to sustain your life style and get rid of the unwanted debt without stressing and worrying about keeping those balls (I mean bills) in the air!

This is our time, ladies; you hold your own keys to unlock your future. Perhaps some of you are still hoping and wishing that your knight in shining armor will appear, and you won't have to build your financial empire yourself.

Nely Galan, self-made media mogul, said two things. The first: "Ladies, there's no Prince Charming!" She was not talking about a mate; she was talking about the fact that a man is not a financial plan. Meghan Markle landed Prince Harry, and whether you have your own Prince Harry or not, you really do hold the keys to design the life you want today and the future you desire tomorrow. Nely said even with her business success, she started investing in real estate and was in the position to retire by the time she was 45. This is possible for you too, and if you are 45 or older, you would be surprised what you can accomplish in five years with the right investment plan. The other thing Nely said was, "Buy buildings, not shoes!"

Let me ask you: Do you have a financial safety net? Do you have a back-up plan for emergencies? Savings that will carry you through for a year or more? What if your child got sick? Could you be off to care for your child without this decision becoming a financial burden? Do you have an investment vehicle that is gaining you passive income?

And for you, students, student loan debt is at an all-time high. Will your interest payments exceed the money you actually borrowed? Because it will take you forever to pay it off. These are the questions we should be asking ourselves, and hopefully, you have a solid financial portfolio in place. Whether you have a solid plan in place or not, keep reading because the rock star real estate investment women and ancillaries in this book will surely open your eyes to more that's available to you.

It's the 21st century; we have more opportunities, access to live life on our terms, and more doors open to us and are in more rooms than ever before. But we are still working to establish ourselves financially and in the work place. Women are still underpaid; sometimes two times less than men. Some of us have even been victims of the 'Me Too' movement, which makes the cost of getting ahead in the workplace way too high. Should we, as women, really have to lower our moral standards in order to get ahead and reach the financial goals that we desire? No. Picking ourselves, empowering ourselves, and acquiring a financial education, along with some major changes that still need to take place in the world, are necessary for us to live the lives we are destined to have.

Even still, the world is our oyster. We not only have the resources to provide for ourselves financially but we also have opportunities available so we don't have to feel chained to our jobs anymore. No job, no position, no man should require us to compromise. We no longer will accept being insulted, undervalued, or taken for granted because we've got choices.

As modern women today, we have to work smarter, not harder, to sustain ourselves, our family, and our future. Job stability is gone. Divorce is at an all-time high, and there are more single women right now than ever before. This doesn't have to be doomsday for us. Actually, the contrary can be true if we not only change our mindset but also our actions and position ourselves to build wealth, and one of the most rewarding ways to accomplish that is through real estate investing.

I challenge you to read each chapter in this short book that features a variety of women who have achieved success through real estate investing. Each chapter is a stand-alone, so if a title intrigues you, read that chapter. But go back and read them all. I'm confident that after reading this book, your perspective will change about the possibilities that are available to you to strengthen or establish a sustainable investment portfolio that includes real estate investments.

Take a moment and think about the answers to these questions:

Do you feel bound to your job because you need the money? Are you earning six figures but feel like you have golden handcuffs? If you got sick tomorrow, could you sustain your life for six months, one year?

What if you could earn a passive income that not only exceeded your working income but would grant you the security you need so that if you ever felt the threat of losing your job or needed money to fund an entrepreneurial venture, it was available in your portfolio? You could be your own bank. You could quit your job or take a leave of absence. You could easily take the time you desire for maternity leave, all without having the stress of wondering how to maintain your lifestyle because you'd be financially secure.

What if you could pay for the education you want your child to have, all without taking a dime away from your current earnings? What if you could go on vacation without feeling guilty about the cost? What if you were able to go out to dinner with your girlfriends and pick up the tab instead of declining to go because of not having enough ready cash available? What if you could still create an incredible retirement income even if your 401(k) lost money, or you're just starting to accumulate money for retirement?

And are you aware of the $30,000,000,000 Great Wealth Transfer said to be coming to women?

What does that mean to you? You need to get a solid financial education so that you can identify great investment opportunities, and this book will expose you to the real estate investment team you need so you are ready to take advantage of opportunities. And you never know; you just may inherit money or other resources from family members and be a part of that great wealth transfer.

Whether you are 20, 30, 40, or older, you need multiple streams of income, and you want some of those streams to be passive.

What we are talking about is lifestyle independence. Real estate investing can afford you these freedoms and more. If you are still not convinced, take a hard look at these statistics:

- One in three Americans have nothing saved for retirement.
- Women are 27% more likely to have no retirement savings.
- 76% of baby boomers aren't confident they've saved enough for retirement.
- 55% of retirees retire earlier than expected. Health was the #No. 1 reason for retiring early, followed by job loss.

Would you like to be in a position to retire when you choose, be it at 40, 50, or 60? And for you, millennial ladies and the many women that have gone back to college and gotten advanced degrees with student debt at an all-time high and social security probably not going to be available much longer, what's your financial game plan?

What if you could learn how women just like you from all walks of life? From CEOs running million-dollar companies to six-figure licensed professionals to a highly successful woman who was raised in foster care; from moms to entrepreneurs; the women featured in these pages can help you to build and sustain wealth.

Whether you are divorced, single, happily married, rebuilding or are currently experiencing no financial challenges at all, it is always wise to include real estate in your financial portfolio, and there are some pretty unique investment opportunities offered in this book:

Ask any millionaire or billionaire, no matter what industry they are in, and they will most likely tell you that their wealth was not built only from their business income, insurance, or the stock market. Real estate investing played a major role in helping a large percentage of the world's millionaires and billionaires obtain wealth. It is an important component of a well-diversified portfolio. This book will open the door to one of the best financial educations you can obtain.

As women, we are always five to ten years ahead of the game, thinking about what's next, how we want to live, what we want to leave for our children and grandchildren. It's time to invest in yourself and in your future. People are living longer and out-living their retirement. If you have more month than money these days, have multiple side hustles, or even if you have a nice salary and feel comfortable today, you should seriously consider learning about the different ways you can invest in real estate in the chapters of this book. Don't let a lack of knowledge or the fear of failing hold you back. Secure your future so your money can out-live you. Real estate investing is an investment that can change your life and the lives of generations to come.

Former first lady Michelle Obama said, "A woman's place is truly wherever she wants it to be. They (women) don't just transform their own lives; they transform the life of this nation and our entire world."

Working less and having more is the goal for most women. So, do yourself a favor. Take a few hours and read through these pages. You are guaranteed to find a professional, a real estate investment strategy, or asset class that you may have never considered investing in.

Success is a team sport, and your team just arrived!

You deserve this. Grab something to drink and explore the possibilities and opportunities in these pages. Happy exploring!

–Lisa Charlene Williams, publisher

Whether You're a Mother, 9–5er, or Just Need Some Side Cash, this is the Income Strategy for You

Do you need to make money ASAP? Well, let the Queen of Mobile Homes help you. Before becoming the Queen of Mobile Homes, life was not easy for Chimene, and her origin screams 'relatability.' Raised in and out of foster care, Chimene beat the odds stacked against her. She worked a corporate 9–5, like many women, before being laid off. She is also a mother of five and a wife.

When laid off, Chimene had a choice to make: follow the corporate world or take a leap of faith into real estate investing. Needless to say, she chose the latter after reading the Purple Bible (real estate investing book), taking a course led by Kim Kiyosaki, and hearing her husband say that he believed in her.

Chimene is now committed and determined to help other women to do the same, as well as college students, single mothers, and corporate executives. She shares her passive investment opportunities that anyone can invest in, which can offer on average a 12% rate of return. With over fifty investors in her portfolio from all walks of life, she is confident that she can help you too. Chimene has discovered the secret to making three thousand to five thousand dollars per day from mobile home investing, and she wants to show you how to do it too.

Conversation with Chimene Van Gundy 'The Queen of Mobile Homes'

Tell us about your company, your focus, and how investing in real estate can change or impact a woman's life.

Chimene Van Gundy: My company is the Queen of Mobile Homes, and I offer turnkey passive investment opportunities, specializing in mobile home real estate investing, which includes fixing and flipping mobile homes as well as wholesaling mobile homes. This is a niche market, but it can work to your advantage because some of these strategies don't require any money or credit to get started.

Essentially, we manage everything: from buying the unit, fixing and flipping it, to finding a buyer for it and putting the deal together. After that, we manage the unit for the term of the note. The industry is owner financing, not rental, so we aren't considered as the landlord of the mobile home. We're not dealing with the toilets, trash, tenants, and termites. We're essentially the bank, which is putting more money into your pocket in the process.

Basically, in my company, we solve three problems: how to invest with a busy mom schedule, how to invest with little or no money, and how to invest without credit. We work with all kinds of women: moms, business women, even the higher professional women. My aim is to teach these women how to be a shark in a blue ocean of mobile homes which is ripe for opportunity.

This can be a niche market, but this is advantageous for multiple reasons: there are not many people in the market, which means that you have more opportunities; it can also be profitable, no matter where you are—meaning that it is the best passive income strategy.

WEALTH FOR WOMEN · 9

What investment opportunities do you offer, and what is typically required for an initial investment?

Chimene Van Gundy: What I do with my clients is to help them invest the minimum amount. They can bring that to me to invest, anywhere between fifteen to twenty thousand dollars. After that, we invest the money into a mobile home unit and begin to turn it around. From this, clients will roughly get a twelve to fifteen-percent return on their investment, which is an amazing amount to make as an offset.

Mobile homes have the potential to make up to four times what a traditional house can make.

Why is investing in real estate advantageous to women?

Chimene Van Gundy: There is an extreme financial benefit in terms of what you could make with mobile homes versus traditional housing. Mobile homes have the potential to make up to four times what a house can make. There's a huge market, an enormous market for affordable housing. I have some statistics here from 2017 that I would like to share—that would show some of the advantages.

According to the National Manufactured housing association, over twenty-two million Americans live in manufactured housing. Mostly, this is due to the average cost of a mobile home being lower than a traditional house. So, you have this huge market. On top of that, you can charge a higher percentage on your mobile home than other forms of housing. Mobile homes in parks are considered personal property, not real estate, so this becomes a huge advantage. You're dealing with people that don't necessarily have stellar credit, right? But everyone must have housing, so it's a win-win situation. While you are providing affordable housing to people that need it, you're also able to get a good rate of return on your investment.

Why would you say it's beneficial for someone interested in mobile home investing, and what is the benefit of working with you?

Chimene Van Gundy: I have wholesaled over a hundred mobile homes. On top of that, I have fixed and flipped over three hundred mobile homes. In the last three years as well, I have been able to take my business international.

Right now, I'm working in Ireland on what they call 'holiday homes': the trend is that within the next fifteen years, the industry will be worth almost a billion dollars in Europe. I think outside of the box, so I'm on the cutting edge of it.

What are the biggest myths when it comes to real estate investing?

Chimene Van Gundy: In my niche, I think the biggest myth and taboo is the thought of 'trailer trash.' Though mobile homes are little boxes that spit out cash, they are like ATMs on wheels. Every day, they are overlooked by the average real estate investor.

Why would you say that now is a good time to invest in real estate? And are some of the receptions we have from the market crash still true for us today?

Chimene Van Gundy: The reason that mobile homes are such a great investment is that they are steady. There are no ups and downs in the market like there are with others. Mobile homes are affordable housing, which is always needed. I like to call mobile homes 'forever cash': people will always need a place to live, and the trend has moved away from apartments being an affordable alternative for people. Harvard released a study back in 2016 that says that in America alone, we are about four to five million units short on housing. So, for me, mobile homes are never going to go away. This makes the market under-tapped and underutilized to be in. In 2008, after the market crashed, the purchase and sales of mobile homes went up 20%.

When it comes to women that are investing in real estate for the first time, what are some of the most common fears or concerns that they have about getting started?

Chimene Van Gundy: "I could never do that"; "I just don't know if I'm smart enough"; "I don't have enough money"; "I don't have the credit"; or "I don't have the time."

I tell people that nobody is busier than me. I have five children; my youngest is four, and my oldest is twenty-three. So, I have a wide range of kids and still have little ones at home now; I know what it's like to be a busy mom. I know what it's like to be the single mom who's gone through the divorce, and it's wreaked havoc on her life.

I don't know if you can imagine what wholesale could do for a mom, but let me give you an example. A lady in Arizona called me, asking advice on how to sell her mobile home. Within forty-eight hours, we had taken the initial investment of $800 and given her a profit of $3,500. So, what I tell people is that it costs literally no money to do this. Essentially, what we are doing is to use a social media strategy, alongside apps, to find mobile homes. Once this is accomplished, we get the contract, assign it to another person and go from there.

The greatest part about this is that you can be in a totally different state and be doing this all day, every day. With that kind of work, you are looking at between three and eight thousand dollars. And you can do this from the comfort of your own home—I will teach you how to do this.

How do you feel that real estate investing makes life better?

Chimene Van Gundy: I started real estate investing in 2015. At that time, I had been working a corporate job, worked my tail off for this company and made them a lot of money. I developed a lot of systems and processes in this division and then was laid off. My husband and I had been married not even two years, and we had four children at home, so I had no idea what I was going to do. I drove home that night scared to tell my husband that I was laid off, but he said four words to me that changed my life. He said, "I believe in you," and I had never heard those four words before, but it changed my life. It sparked something in me. At that point in time, I needed my children to know that I could take care of them, that 'a man is not a plan.' I needed them to know that I was going to see that their needs were met and that they would have this belief in me. They needed that structure, that love and confidence that I was going to make sure that we could keep that standard of living we had been at.

I grew up in and out of foster care and was abused by the system. When out, I was one of seven children and was often forgotten and told I was unwanted. I married beforehand and then got a divorce. When a woman gets divorced, her quality of life goes down by eighty percent, whereas a man is not affected so much. So, I'm here because I'm the mother of three girls; for my girls, this is dear to me. I am in a man's world, and I must work twice as hard to get recognized. But, you know, that's okay because when this movement happens, and we empower women, then we will create a generational change. This is the purpose of this book, and it is also the purpose of Queen of Mobile Homes. My goal, ultimately, is to make a thousand women a million dollars to start this generational change in the world. Just imagine what that would mean for a thousand families for generations. You make one woman a millionaire, and she will affect the next 5 generations.

So, when my husband said this, I got more confidence in myself. I ended up reading *Rich Dad, Poor Dad*, known as the Purple Bible, right? I found out that they had an introductory course over Mother's Day weekend that year and sold some of my belonging to pay for the package that included a mentor. My mentor came to visit in the next month—June or July of 2015—and in a matter of four months, I had almost made $200,000.

I tell people this because this is the difference that it makes. I'm here to tell people that I will be their coach and mentor; I will be the one who says, "I believe in you." I want them to move their lives forward because their success is my success. Real estate investing can change your life. It took me from a negative $50,000 to a net worth of over a million dollars in less than 18 months.

Can you share a success story that you have about someone that you have worked with?

Chimene Van Gundy: Absolutely. So, I have a student that I am coaching right now out of Georgia. He was in the real estate fix and flip division for about twenty years, but that was a lot to manage. You know, you can really lose out on a lot of income when you're dealing with houses. So, I worked with him and taught him a lot of the strategies that we use to price mobile homes and make sure that we are getting the best deal. Now, since we were able to put the amount of money that he normally puts into fix-and-flips into mobile home units, he was able to triple his income. Today, he has completely stepped away from fixing and flipping homes to doing the same with mobile homes in the Georgia area.

What originally interested you in mobile home investing?

Chimene Van Gundy: I have a B.A. in Criminal Justice, so I had worked as a paralegal for years for different companies and attorneys. So, I understand contracts very well, and I was going to tax sales and meeting investors. After talking to them for a while, I would share my background, and they would eventually ask for advice on a mobile home with a title issue or something else. I took home three mobile home deals and was able to work through them in a matter of days. After some time, I started getting hundreds of leads and thought, *Oh my gosh, I have something now.* So, that's when I turned to wholesale mobile homes and started making money per signed agreement.

Eventually, though, I read *Deals on Wheels* by Lonnie Scruggs and spent some time fine-tuning the message of owner financing. That's when I really realized that mobile homes are little boxes that spit out cash.

What is one lesson that you learned early on as an investor that you think makes you a more valuable person to work with today?

Chimene Van Gundy: One lesson that I learned early on is that the definition of insanity is doing the same thing twice and expecting a different result.

I knew if I wanted to live the life that I desired and wanted to gain financial independence, I had to do something differently. So, I followed my coach and mentor and did what they said and changed my mindset. So, one thing I've learned is to get a coach, especially if you don't have a lot of time, money, or credit; these things can all make the mistakes costly. Not only that but if you have a coach, you can cut your learning time in half.

What do you think is the most important question that a woman should ask herself as she considers where she is today, where she wants to be tomorrow or a year from now, and what she can do to ensure that she gets there?

Chimene Van Gundy: I think the most important question is if they are happy where they are. Is this what they saw for themselves? Is this where they imagined they would be at fifteen or twenty? "Who am I depending on for security?" (Because 'a man is not a plan.')

I think, again, that the biggest hurdle that anyone faces is their mindset. This is our self-doubt or self-belief. Really, we create anything that we want to create, but it might be difficult. We might have to sacrifice, but that means that we want more: we aren't OK with mediocrity and are willing to sacrifice today to live a better tomorrow. And I think that's really what you should ask yourself, what you should ensure that you have a grasp on.

I tell all my clients to do a life assessment on themselves to see where they are, where they want to be, and how to formulate a plan to get there. So, what mobile homes provide—and what the Queen of Mobile Homes does—is provide the opportunity for them to get into a niche market that not a lot of people are in. It also means that they get big opportunities and will be able to establish a name for themselves in the market and in the niche.

The last thing that I would say that they needed to ask is if this person that they want to work with—their mission statement—aligns with their core values. I want to say that you should always work with someone whose core values align with your own.

What are three qualities that you would recommend a woman look for when choosing a real estate investor to work with?

Chimene Van Gundy: I think that first, you must ask where you are starting from. Everyone starts from a different place, so they need to really know what it looks like where they are starting from. After this, there are three questions that you should ask yourself when getting to know the person.

"Do they align with my core values?" "Do I connect with this person?" "Is this person someone that I can relate to, and is this person sitting where I want to be?" If the answer to these questions is yes, then this is someone that you should work with.

So, what would you say to a woman who says, "I already make six figures, and I'm doing well for myself," or who thinks that they are too busy? Why would you tell her that she should still consider adding real estate investing to her portfolio?

Chimene Van Gundy: I think the big problem comes from trading your time for money. In real estate, generally, you are making your money work for you, which creates your wealth. Whatever you do, if you aren't working for yourself, then you are trading your time for dollars.

I always like to share a few thoughts with clients. First, I want them to remember that it does not matter where you come from; all that matters is where you're going. The women in this book are here to help women create, to help them turn their passion into action and propel them forward to live the life of their dreams. You should remember that when someone says something is impossible, the word itself means 'I am possible.'

Where can we find out more about you and your real estate investment opportunities?

Chimene Van Gundy: You can find out more about me through my website: QueenOfMobileHomes.com. You can also find me under that name 'Queen of Mobile Homes' on Facebook or my group home, Mobile Home Millions. Mobile Home Millions also happens to be the name of my class.

About Chimene Van Gundy

Company: Queen of Mobile Homes

Who I can help: I help single moms, professional and executive women, and women who no longer want to have to depend on a 'man' for financial freedom.

What sets me apart: What sets me apart in my industry is that there really is no 'expert' on mobile homes and no one else that is going to teach others how they can start with no money and no credit.

Testimonial: "Chimene provided me with the best knowledge in the industry. Her knowledge level will blow your mind! She even gets under the mobile homes with you and teaches you what to look for. I closed 4 deals in 5 days with her. She is really all about her students having success." –Michael T.

How to get in touch with me:

Email: chimene@queenofmobilehomes.com

Website: QueenOfMobileHomes.com

Social Media:

Facebook: Facebook.com/QueenOfMobileHomes

Group page: Facebook.com/MobileHomeMillions

Scan here to learn more:

An Investment Approach Designed for Women where Your Passive Income Can Exceed Your Working Income

Are you a career or professional woman who wants more time and money, whose plate is full and can't seem to figure out how to create more income and stop trading your time for money? Would you like to know how to make your money work for you, instead of you working for your money, and learn in a feminine way? Monick Halm, the real estate investor goddess, can help you. Monick was once in the same position: with a blossoming career as a full-time attorney. On the outside, she had it all, a six-figure income, prestige, but she was on the hamster wheel and miserable. Monick turned to real estate investing and now owns over 1,200 units in six states with her syndication group, spanning apartment buildings, mobile home parks, RV parks, and more. Monick offers a 'Women Only' education and mentorship program designed specifically for women, both new and experienced investors. Learn to invest like a woman and think like an investor. Monick works with women from across the country and is helping them create a life where their passive income investments exceed their working income. If you feel like you have golden handcuffs tying you to your job, learn how you can put yourself in a position to continue to work if you want—but if you don't want to, you don't have to.

Conversation with Monick Halm

Tell us about your company, your focus, and how investing in real estate can enhance, change and positively impact a woman's life.

Monick Halm: My company, Real Estate Goddesses, works with professional females that wish to create a passive income stream through real estate investing. We work with these ladies to create real wealth, a strong relationship, and cultivate their portfolio in a way that they can live the lifestyle that they desire and can make the massive difference on the planet that they were put here to do.

In addition to an online community and podcast, we offer an education and mentoring program, which is designed to educate women about real estate investing and steer them toward the right investments and decisions on their real estate investment journey. The entire coaching program is designed to help women reach out of the confusion and paralyzing fear that can come with investing in real estate and get them back onto the light-filled path that will create their passive income.

In my experience, a lot of women feel that they don't know exactly what to do when starting in real estate investment. I teach them the steps that will help them successfully invest, along with helping them develop the mindset that will afford them confidence and help them get the most out of any situation they might find themselves in.

When working with me, women can create passive income streams with real estate while also setting themselves up for long-term financial well-being, setting the goals and smashing them. This helps to ensure that they will be able to take the time to do whatever they want as well, whether it be quitting their jobs and traveling or just being able to spend more time with their children. To those ends, I also work with these women to collapse their timeframes, to get them on their financial track much more quickly than they would be able to do on their own—all while avoiding costly mistakes to which many first-time real estate investors can fall prey. Due to my long history of working in real estate investment as well, I can help women access the investment opportunities that they might not be able to get into otherwise and guide them along the way.

I believe that investing in real estate is beneficial to women in many ways. I think that through this work, the women can generate their passive income which can either supplement or replace their working income. This can lead them to stop trading their time for dollars and having the set goals for their financial freedom. It also means that they can have an emergency fund if something comes up— either a medical bill or a bigger, more life-changing problem. It means that they can spend more time with their children when they feel that they need to. It also means that they have an established retirement fund, that will not be tied to a job that they hate and grind away at just for the benefits. There are just so many ways that real estate investing can help women with reaching their financial well-being goals.

What aspects of real estate investing do you help clients with?

Monick Halm: I help women successfully navigate each step of the process, including education, searching for properties, teaching them how to do their due diligence, purchase, and manage the assets. I work with them from the beginning of the steps to eventually being able to sell the property.

What kind of return on investment would you say that your clients will receive, and how long does it typically take them to recoup their initial investment?

Monick Halm: Often, my clients can double their invested money in as little as three to five years, but their results depend on them and their goals. I say that real estate investing is not one size fits all, so I help women figure out where they want to end up and what they must do to reach their dream life.

After that, we reverse-engineer their investments to meet their goals—not just by telling us how much they make but by helping them figure out how much work they must do to get their desired return.

What would you say or why would you say your role as a coach is important to someone who is starting to invest in real estate?

Monick Halm: Education is the most important thing for success in real estate. What you don't know will end up costing you.

I provide education to women, and I help them collapse their timeframes and avoid costly mistakes. I think that it's crucial, then, to have a coach or a mentor through this process. There's a lot to know about the real estate game, and over the thirteen years that I've been investing, I've both learned a lot and made a lot of mistakes. It's those mistakes, plus those of my mentors, that I bring to my clients because they can leverage off that. I want to make sure that my clients do not have the same expensive mistakes that I've had to deal with.

What type of challenges do you help your clients prevent that could possibly occur during a real estate transaction?

Monick Halm: I think that the worst thing is when you don't know what you don't know and when you've missed crucial warning signs or opportunities. I help women avoid those pitfalls, and I also help them find the value-added opportunities. I help them find ways in which they could do better than they might even know was possible— but also not lose money by missing something important.

For someone who is starting off on real estate investing, why would you tell them it's important that they have a real estate mentor? And what are three qualities you would recommend they look for?

Monick Halm: I would tell them that yes, you can do it yourself, but it's going to take a lot longer, and you're more likely to make expensive mistakes. You'll also likely miss out on an opportunity that is staring right at you but that you can't see.

When I was just starting out in real estate, I thought you had to start with one house and then buy another and then buy another until you had a large portfolio. My big goal was to get a 4-plex. But I had a great mentor that suggested instead of going small and being limited to my own capital and credit, I could bring a group of investors together and buy a 100- or 200-unit building. I didn't even know this was a possibility! I hired him as a mentor, and I followed these steps. Within a year, instead of that 4-plex, I ended up with over 1,000 units.

So, really, it made an exceptional difference. You can do it yourself, but you will be missing things. And real estate is generally the most expensive investment you will ever make. If you're spending tens of thousands, hundreds of thousands of dollars, you want to make sure you're doing it right. I've seen so many people lose their shirts, and that's the last thing that I want to see for any woman who has worked hard for her money. I think that's why you need to have a mentor.

How can real estate investing help someone's life?

Monick Halm: There are so many ways: replace your salary, fund your retirement, create a nest egg, leave a legacy for your family. It also allows you to have the freedom to start or grow a business, fund your child's college education, living the dream that you want to live but that you might miss out on when trapped by your jobs. There's so much that comes with real estate investing, but it boils down to basically a real estate investment that can help you create both financial and time freedom. And with that, you have the extra money and time and can live the life that you want to live.

Do you have a success story that you could share?

Monick Halm: I had a client who owned a yoga studio. Her husband was an executive at a tech company. They had a good income, but as she looked down the line, she realized that if she stopped working, she wouldn't be making money. She had no plan for retirement and would have to keep working or really reduce her lifestyle. She came to me and told me that she wanted to create a passive income through real estate. So I helped her buy her first duplex that she then rented out, and undertake several flips to bring in more cash. I was able to help her keep adding to her portfolio. After about two-and-a-half years, they now have seventeen rental doors, and she has more than enough passive income to completely replace her yoga income and is currently about two-thirds of the way through replacing her husband's income. Now, they are almost financially free and can work or not work as they choose.

What inspired you to become a real estate educator and mentor?

Monick Halm: When I first started investing, I met a man—a mentor—who opened my mind to the idea of bringing a group of investors together to purchase properties. This exponentially shifted what I was able to do with real estate by hiring him as a mentor. At that time, I realized that we can't do it alone, especially since I was entrusted with other people's money. It's one thing to lose your own money, but to lose another people's money? For me, it's the most terrifying possible thing in the world.

So, now, I'm always learning. I'm always educating myself to get better by going to conferences and learning everything that I can. I often go to conferences, and ninety percent of the room are men—but no one on the stage is a woman, and women are little unicorns that pop up here and there. I wanted to shape that and invite other women to join because I know that ninety percent of millionaires in this country are created through real estate, and this is the best way to build wealth. But nobody is speaking to women, showing them how this is done. We as women do not think or move or invest the same way that men do. We have differences that tend to make us better investors and have, on average, better results than men if only we have the courage to get up and do it. I am inspired, then, to help women get into the game in a way that feels good to them and creates the best possible results.

Could you recall a lesson that you learned early on when you began real estate investing that shaped how you see your work today? And what makes you a more valuable mentor to work with?

Monick Halm: As I mentioned before, one of the main lessons I've learned is, I don't invest in a way that is reliant on my own capital and credit but doing it in a better, more resourceful way. I'm working with OPM (Other People's Money) and OPT (Other People's Time). It's win-win, as I'm able to help others grow their money while also growing mine and leveraging my time. So, that was a huge lesson that I've learned over the course of many years.

I've learned tons of other lessons over the years through my mistakes. In my podcast, I interview successful female real estate investors. I always ask them what their number one mistake was and what they learned from it. Through my own and my guests' mistakes, I've discovered that you learn the most when things go wrong. All that I've learned helps me become a more valuable mentor.

What questions should a woman ask herself when she thinks about where she is today, where she wants to be tomorrow, and how she can achieve those goals?

Monick Halm: A lot of women don't ask themselves where they want to be, which is the most important thing to ask yourself. You must ask where you want to be when you're retiring or where you want to be when you abandon your life. I think you also must ask yourself, *What would I look like if I'm living my best life?* and use that as a springboard to reverse-engineer what you want to do with that.

What three qualities would you recommend someone look for when choosing a mentor or educator?

Monick Halm: One of the most brilliant women that I know and love, Beth Clifford, gave me some advice about what to look for when hiring somebody. Look for the three Cs: Character; Commitment; and Capacity.

As for character, you want somebody with the right character. You want someone with integrity, who is honest, who does what they say that they will.

The next thing to look for is commitment. How committed is this person to your best interest? How committed are they to helping you be the most successful real estate investor possible?

The third stands for 'capacity.' This has to do with the skill level. Has this person actually done what you want them to do? If so, they can teach you how to walk the path in terms of being an investor.

So, those three are what you're looking for: character, commitment, and capacity. And that's something to look for in anybody that you work with—they need all three.

What would you like to say to the woman who is interested in real estate investing?

Monick Halm: I want to tell them to do it! Go for it! We need more women owning the world, and we need more women coming into this business. Before you get started, get educated, get a mentor, but don't get stuck with your wheels turning. Get support so you can take effective action in building wealth for yourself in real estate.

Where can someone contact you?

Monick Halm: They can connect with me at www.realestateinvestorgoddesses.com.

About Monick Halm

Company:
Real Estate Investor Goddesses

Who I can help:
We work with professional females that desire to create passive income streams through real estate investing—to create real wealth, live the lifestyle that they desire and make the massive difference on the planet that they came here to make.

Monick Halm is a real estate investor, syndicator and developer who has over thirteen years of real estate investing in multiple areas, including multi-family, mobile home parks, RV parks, vacation rentals, and ground-up development. Together with her husband, Monick owns over 1,200 rental units in six states. Monick is a best-selling author of *The Real Estate Investor Goddess Handbook* and the host of the Real Estate Investor Goddesses Podcast. She is also a Real

Estate Strategy Mentor, a Huffington Post contributor, a keynote speaker, yoga teacher, wife and mother to three amazing kids.

What sets me apart:

I help women successfully create passive income streams through real estate investing in a way that's distinctly feminine.

Testimonial:

"Before working with Monick, I didn't know where to start to make the best use of my time and resources to learn how to invest in my first property. With her help, I am now able to distinguish a good real estate investment deal from a poor one, have confidence in my ability to become an investor, and know how to do it the feminine way. And as a result, I landed my first real estate investment deal, and I expect my second property deal will not be too far off in my future. My advice for those thinking to work with Monick and Real Estate Investor Goddesses is, be prepared to make wonderful new connections, to let go of the masculine paradigm, and to open to the feminine way to create true wealth and prosperity." –Melissa P.

How to get in touch with me:

Email: monick@realestateinvestorgoddesses.com
Website: RealEstateInvestorGoddesses.com

Social Media:
Twitter.com/monickpaulhalm
Facebook.com/RealEstateInvestorGoddesses

Scan here to learn more:

A Sound Investment Starts with Getting the Right Loan

So you've decided that real estate investing may be a good idea, but where do you start? How much will you qualify for? What does it take to secure an investment property loan? And what is the difference between owner-occupied financing and non-owner-occupied financing? These are all concerns that an experienced mortgage lender, like Caeli Ridge, President and CEO (and fellow investor like yourself) of Ridge Lending Group, can help you with.

From the mortgage market crash to predatory lending like never before, it is so important to work with a seasoned and respected professional, especially when it comes to your mortgage.

Caeli is one of the premier voices on non-owner-occupied funding, is licensed around the country and can help you with both residential and commercial transactions. Caeli understands mortgages from both the lending side and as an investor. She has held as many as 42 properties at one time across the country and has worked in every capacity. Mortgage lending is in Caeli's blood; she is a 2nd generation lender with over 20 years of mortgage experience; her father founded RLG. If you want to qualify for the most you can and get the safest mortgage, along with educational training and expert strategic advice, look no further. Keep reading.

Conversation with Caeli Ridge

Caeli, you're a mortgage lender that specializes in residential non-owner-occupied funding. Tell us about your company and the benefits a woman would receive working with you.

Caeli Ridge: RLG is a second generation company specializing in investors and their lending needs, whether that be conventional, specialty, commercial, or a fix/flip. We're licensed nationwide and can boast a highly skilled team of a combined 60+ years of experience in working with investors. Most importantly, I am a RE-investor, having held 42 properties at any one time across the United States. The fact that I am a woman that has succeeded in a largely male-dominated space allows me to support the education of women from a unique perspective—and from the lending side of the equation.

One of the most crucial things we do is educating investors on how to optimize their qualifications from a lending and underwriting point of view. We teach investors the definitions and guidelines, learn what their goals are and structure the leverage of these investments around those most important details.

When you work with a mortgage lender like us, you gain a truly deep understanding of lending as it applies specifically to you as an individual and your qualifications/goals. We create a roadmap together that helps you navigate a very detailed and often overwhelming or intimidating process of lending. Because, let's face it, without the leverage usage, our ROIs are a fraction of what they would be by using OPM (other people's money).

Working with a mortgage lender like RLG, you gain control or understanding of the finance side of the puzzle that is very empowering—it allows an individual to scale in a way that would never be possible by using their own capital alone.

What aspects of the real estate investing process do you help clients with?

Caeli Ridge: Of course, we help with lending, anywhere in the country you might be. Beyond that, we help clients with strategic planning and sequencing of sorts to figure out what their trajectory and goals are and plan accordingly. We also offer mentorship and education to investors.

What is different about you from others that offer your services?

Caeli Ridge: To my knowledge, there is not another mortgage lender in the country that has the experience (led by a fellow investor), nationwide footprint and that provides the education we do for our investors. We are very unique in our space of MTG (mortgage) lending.

I've heard that real estate investing is a team sport. Why is your role an important part of the process?

Caeli Ridge: As mentioned previously, it's the leverage you can achieve through real estate that creates the greatest rate of return on your investment. Beyond all the additional value-add RLG offers, the loan that you will secure on each of your investment properties is one of the most important aspects of successful reinvesting. Our role is key.

What types of challenges can you help prevent that can occur during a real estate transaction?

Caeli Ridge: Well, among other things, RLG takes our clients through a rigorous PQ process that allows us to avoid any unnecessary 'brain damage' once we have a 'live transaction.' Because much of the work we do is upfront, the result is a foregone conclusion, and we can count on closing.

The world has become a DIY society. We can be our own everything. Why is it important for someone who is embarking on a real estate investment opportunity to work with a mortgage lender that specializes in residential non-owner-occupied loans?

Caeli Ridge: MTG lending is an extremely exhaustive, very detailed process. And that's just for a primary residence. Make that an investment property, and we're talking 10 fold. It's taken me 20+ years and lots of trial and error to understand how to effectively navigate the battleship in a creek—that analogy should paint the appropriate picture. You likely don't want to navigate on your own.

Can you describe your typical client to us? Who are you used to working with, and what can you offer that group of people?

Caeli Ridge: Usually, our investors are going to be professionals between the ages of 30 and 70 years old. Most of them are still in the workforce; generally, we'll see a husband and wife team who are looking to achieve some financial freedom through passive, long-term buy-and-hold real estate investments. They've got liquidity. Usually, they come with pretty good credit and a solid debt-to-income ratio. Like I said before, financing in all of this can be a little overwhelming and sometimes intimidating. So we want to focus a good amount of our attention on helping them *understand* some of the 'why' behind the 'how,' right?

So, what we'll do is, we'll take them, and we'll give them definitions of the underwriting guidelines specifically as it applies to them and their qualifications. And then beyond that, we're going to teach them how to optimize those qualifications in relation to what their short- and long-term goals are and kind of package it up and prepare them for what's next, tomorrow, next year, and in five years. That's very different than a traditional lender, yes?

I want to focus on it because you don't know what you don't know. And I've got clients that prior to having some of these discovery conversations maybe would have filed their Schedule E, for example, in a certain way that would have precluded them qualifying for a whole year until the next tax return was due, and we give them that guidance and that education.

How do you deliver that type of education?

Caeli Ridge: You know, I've considered some of the more technological formats of providing this, but right now, it's one-on-one with me personally. We have a mentorship program called Ridge Education and Mentorship Program that we offer to our investor clients that I think they would say they find very valuable.

The content usually goes like this: We'll schedule out between two and four different sessions—which are 30, 40 minutes each—and in each session, we get into the higher level information, the depths of what their qualifications are, the definitions of what that means from UW perspectives, and again show them how to optimize those qualifications.

Secondarily, we look at draft tax returns so that we can advise them prior to the filing; how that Schedule E (which is where the rental properties will fall on a federal tax return) might be affecting qualification. Going forward, then, we'll give them the appropriate advice. Some extremely helpful strategy sessions are included in this mentorship as well.

As a mortgage lender, what kind of concerns can you help a new real estate investor avoid?

Caeli Ridge: Because of my background and experience, I'm able to offer my thoughts and devil's advocate on market conditions, appropriate diversification, property returns, independent turnkeys, and the like.

We're looking for some practical advice—where should people invest in the US?

Caeli Ridge: Well, let's assume they are looking for cash flow since that's where most people's focus is right now. The highest cash flow I'm seeing is going to be in states like Ohio, Indiana, Alabama, Oklahoma, Tennessee, and Missouri.

The appreciation typically is reserved for the Sunbelt states. Now they have a solid cash flow, but you'll find as an investor, usually the higher the cash flow, the lower the appreciation and vice versa, right? The higher the appreciation, the more modest the cash flow. But the Sunbelt states—the Carolinas, Florida, Georgia, Texas—those states are going to be usually the ones that have the better long-term pay for appreciation.

What inspired you to become a mortgage lender, and why do you have a focus on residential non-owner-occupied funding?

Caeli Ridge: My father was the founder. He retired in 2009 officially. I have been at the helm, though, since 2005. We kind of found ourselves in a space around the early 2000s where we were competing in the mortgage industry for other owner-occupied business, and it was pretty harsh. So, we looked at other ways to differentiate ourselves, and maybe a little bit by default, we came across an individual that was doing lots of volume of non-owner-occupied purchases and resales. So, that piqued our interest. And long story short, we just took it and ran with it. I became the authority on the lending side of non-owner-occupied. After weathering some pretty difficult storms along the way, we became investors ourselves. We focus on education, and throughout the last 20 years, Ridge Lending has been the preferred lender for dozens of different turnkeys nationwide.

What drives you? Tell us about your passion for what you do and the people you help.

Caeli Ridge: I sincerely enjoy working with investors and being a part of their support team to creating great wealth through real estate.

How has your experience as a woman in this particularly male-dominated industry shaped you and your business?

Caeli Ridge: I've been very lucky. Lucky as a woman by having some very powerful male mentors, and those men in my life have just been invaluable to me. While I don't want to short side men, I do want to focus on where I feel my most powerful and my most useful self, which is in the relationships that I have been able to form with other like-minded women. I'm in a position to help impart some of my knowledge and my own sense of self and maybe some of my confidence in women that are up and coming and they want to find their own voice and their own place and purpose in this world. Nothing could be more fulfilling.

What's the most important question women should ask themselves as they consider where they are today, where they want to be tomorrow, and how they plan to get there?

Caeli Ridge: "Who am I going to surround myself with to help elevate my success and my goals of total financial independence? And where do I find them?"

What questions would you ask women in particular while you're working with them?

Caeli Ridge: My first questions would be about fact finding; are we looking at cash flow exclusively? Are we looking at cash flow and a little appreciation? Are we looking more at appreciation? What about tax benefits?

What three qualities would you recommend a woman reading your chapter consider when choosing a mortgage lender to work with?

Caeli Ridge: Experience.

Nationwide licensing.

Experience (it's *that* important!).

In closing, what would you like to say to a woman interested in real estate investing?

Caeli Ridge: In my experience, women have amazing instincts. Trust your intuition and surround yourself with the best team.

About Caeli Ridge

Company: Ridge Lending Group

Who I can help: RLG has worked with investors and homeowners alike in investing in and purchasing both commercial and residential properties. If you're looking to secure a loan in any of these areas and gain invaluable mentorship and education along the way, RLG is a good fit for you.

What sets me apart: RLG boasts 60+ years of combined experience, for which there is really no replacement. While leading the industry in both technology and education, RLG is committed to using that extensive knowledge and experience to mentor and educate clients in a way that is unseen anywhere else.

Testimonial: "Caeli and Ridge Lending Group have a firm understanding of what real estate investors need in the lending process. Ridge has successfully helped investors in my network get started on the path to cash flow and durable passive income." –Keith Weinhold, Get Rich Education

"The team at Ridge Lending Group has been a cornerstone of my professional success. Always prompt, professional, and courteous, they are also experts in mortgage financing and tax law. They make the process of buying investment homes painless, and they are a joy to work with. I will continue to use them in the future to expand my own real estate holdings, and I highly recommend them to anyone else who desires to start or grow their own investment portfolio."
–J. Gallagher and family

How to get in touch with me:
Phone: 855-74-RIDGE (74343)
Email: INFO@RIDGELENDINGGROUP.COM
Website: WWW.RIDGELENDINGGROUP.COM

Social Media:
Facebook: @RidgeLending
Twitter: @Ridge_Lending
LinkedIn: Ridge Lending Group

Scan here to learn more:

Think Bigger, Invest with a Team

Do you assume only big businesses and large corporations own apartment buildings? Have you ever wondered if it's possible to devote your time and money to real estate investing when you can't seem to get away from work? Laure Marmontel knows exactly what you're thinking, and she helps professional women every day to invest money with small risk and high rewards. Through her firm, Laure has amassed over 1,000+ units through the acquisition of apartment buildings, and her lessons and myth busters on acquiring these will help you find your own real estate investing success.

Laure is a master of finances, real estate strategies and more and has built a committed team and helps others leverage their resources to achieve financial success. Laure's caring approach to making investing a win-win for everyone is why she's achieved such great success. The real estate investing entry point doesn't have to be just single-family homes and owning a second home. Laure will show you how to think bigger and reap greater profits. If you have been trying to figure out how to create additional income without picking up a second job, passive income investments in 'multi-family' real estate in the Southern states might be just what you are looking for.

Conversation with Laure Marmontel

What is your company name, and what do you do?

Laure Marmontel: My name is Laure Marmontel, and I am one of the founders of Cornerstone Investment Partners, LLC, out of Florida.

How do you help someone with regard to real estate investing?

Laure Marmontel: Busy professionals with 9-to-5 jobs or who bill by the hour, who can't devote their time to searching for properties, doing due diligence or managing them. Since we are specialized in cash-flowing group investments, we are able to present them with 'ready-to-invest' opportunities. This allows them to take advantage of the benefits of investing in real estate and to participate in the ownership of multi-family properties that would otherwise be out of reach to them individually.

What is your asset class or area of specialty?

Laure Marmontel: We invest in apartment complexes, usually no older than the 1980s–1990s construction—they generate comfortable cash flow and offer an opportunity to increase their value. We like to buy those assets in the Southern states because the laws are usually more landlord friendly and the economy there has been stronger.

Where do you invest? What type of investments have you invested in?

Laure Marmontel: We focus on investing in rental apartment complexes, also called 'multi-families,' usually between 60 to 300 units. We have vested interest and ownership in approx. 120 million dollars in asset value. The reason we've decided to specialize in 'multi-families' is that we have invested in various other types of assets—like a 120-boat slip marina and RV campground that we turned into a 'Glamping resort,' which we repositioned and outfitted with cute, tiny home cabins on Lake Wylie in Charlotte, North Carolina; a hotel; 2 office complexes and retail in New York—and a rental apartment is something that people will always need, and that's what we're focusing on.

Who is your ideal investor?

Laure Marmontel: Our ideal investor is a busy professional who bills by the hour, dentist, CPA, or busy executive that knows if they take time off work, they're not making money. These professionals love our 'ready-to-invest' solutions for them. They continue billing their clients and meanwhile make good returns passively with us while having peace of mind.

What type of success can you help your investors or clients achieve?

Laure Marmontel: The success is in investing in multi-families, therefore offering diversification and mitigating risk, compared to more fluctuating investments like the stock market. Their hard-earned capital is better preserved and not likely to disappear in an Enron or Lehman Brothers type of crash. Our income-producing properties generate multiple streams of income under one roof and offer economies of scale. Returns on investments vary by project, and that's why we have a personal conversation with each investor discussing their needs and expectations and the fit between us.

What's unique about you as a professional or investor that's different from others who offer similar services?

Laure Marmontel: We are different because we care, and we live by the philosophy of we "Do Whatever It Takes." I began my career as a passive investor, and I know what it feels like, especially as a woman. When I wanted to get started in real estate, I really didn't know where to turn, and there wasn't any place to get guidance, information, or education, except becoming a real estate agent and a mortgage broker—both of which I did in Florida in the 2000s.

Later, I discovered 'multi-families,' and the light bulb went on, "Oh, that's the perfect way to create wealth in real estate." So, from being in that position, I know how to take care of my investors and of our investments.

Can you share how many projects you're involved in?

Laure Marmontel: Well, we have that Charlotte, NC marina/glamping resort mentioned above. We have a great smaller multi-family in Tulsa, Oklahoma, right on the river next to the University and Hospital. It's also right by the new park that was just built for almost 500 million dollars—location, location, location! We have only one apartment complex left in Texas, of 172 units, after maximizing our investors' profits by selling off our 3 Texas apartment complexes, totaling 624 units. We just closed on our third apartment complex of the year in the Atlanta, Georgia market for a total of 170 units.

Laure, tell us about your company, your focus, and how investing in real estate can enhance, change and positively impact a woman's life.

Laure Marmontel: We've been operating for 10 years. We have decided to focus on apartment complexes that were built from the mid-80s on, located in the Southern states, as this is a niche that we feel has many advantages, is steadier and offers good upside potential. Great returns are fantastic, and capital preservation is very important too.

What types of investment opportunities do you offer, and how much is required for an initial investment?

Laure Marmontel: In our multi-family group investments (actually called 'syndications'), the minimum investment is usually 50,000 dollars. Then during our ownership of the property, we give the investors the lion's share of the cash flow, usually paid quarterly. When we sell the property, investors receive their original investment back in addition to the majority of the profits. Profits come from the increase in value and equity that we generated for them during the time we owned and managed the property.

Why is investing in real estate advantageous to women and specifically 1980s–1990s apartment complexes?

Laure Marmontel: Well, it is said that 90 percent of millionaires were made in real estate. So, why not us, right?

First, it's about tax advantages. Because we structure our opportunities professionally and each property is owned by a separate LLC, we can pass to our investors the advantages of real estate ownership, e.g., depreciation and overall positive tax treatment.

We look for markets with vibrant growing economies. Then we look for under-managed multi-family properties that have strong potential for rent increase after the renovation of their outdated units and/or because their current rents are below markets.

1980s–1990s apartment complexes offer that potential and allow us to generate comfortable returns to our lady investors.

And what is the benefit of working with you as an investor?

Laure Marmontel: We have been in your shoes as passive investors; we understand you. We also have a strong track record of providing our investors great returns. As we do so, we do it mindfully.

We care about our tenants, we care about the environment, we care about our investors, and we care about our team.

I remember in one of our earlier projects, a 26-unit apartment complex, upon new ownership of the property, 90 percent of the tenants would have lost their rent subsidies from the government and been unable to pay their rent. We were heartbroken; we had met these tenants when we did the inspection—single women with young children, 90+-year-old retired ladies, a Vietnam vet with health issues who only had 2 cans of beans in his pantry ... So, we fought for them and worked for more than six months with the government agencies to ensure these tenants would be granted new rent subsidies and stay home. So, yes, we are happy when our investors make money, and we make sure we do it right by everyone in a sustainable and ethical way. Everybody benefits. And it's good Karma too!

What do you feel are the biggest myths when it comes to investing in real estate?

Laure Marmontel: Ahah, great question. And yes, I was a victim of these myths for the longest time. I always thought that in order to invest in real estate, you had to buy an investment home and rent it out. I didn't know that regular people like us could buy apartment complexes. But I know better now, and so do you!

What are some common misconceptions around the real estate industry, especially since the 2008 market crash, that are not true today? And why is now a good time to invest in real estate?

Laure Marmontel: Misconceptions ... Hmmm ... That the only way for you to make money in real estate is: buy a house and flip it or rent it out; or buy a home, build equity by paying the mortgage down and letting time increase its value.

What the crash showed us is that it's important to not speculate. And that's why we love cash-flowing apartment complexes. 50+ units under the same roof mitigates the risk of occupancy, bad payers, and allows for economies of scale. And people will always need a roof. We know what our financial break-even point is. We know that in the event of a downturn, we can still pay the mortgage and ride it out.

Also, you are at the mercy of comparables to determine the value of single-family homes. But an apartment complex's value is more stable, as it is based on the income it generates, and you can control that.

Currently, the demand for the type of units we offer is increasing, as the economy is growing. Because of the diverse nature of market cycles, it is also possible to find good investment markets, even in a slowing down economy. No matter what, right now is the best time to invest because "time is money," and money in a 0.5% interest rate savings account or in sleepy IRA doesn't serve you.

What are some of the most common fears you have found that women have about getting started in real estate investing?

Laure Marmontel: "It's going to suck up all of my time, my energy." "I don't have the knowledge." "I don't have the experience." "I'm a woman; they (the Men) are going to take advantage of me." "I don't have enough money to really make it worth it."

All of these factors combine; you are in paralysis by analysis. Pick an investment professional and get all your questions answered. Chatting is not committing. "Date before you get married" is how I like to put it!

How can real estate investing make life better?

Laure Marmontel: Cash Flow! And no worries. And when you're going to retire, you're going to have a nice little nest egg, which could grow even faster if you invest through an IRA. And if one currently doesn't have the capital to invest but has a specific knowledge that can be applied to real estate, one can also participate in the real estate riches by offering their services to professionals like us.

How can you help a woman who is interested in real estate investments achieve the greatest success?

Laure Marmontel: We make sure we educate them so they understand what they're looking at when analyzing an investment opportunity. We discuss their situation and life goals so that they feel confident they're making the best choice in choosing the right opportunity that fits and supports their goals.

Can you share a story about one of your investors and a success they accomplished investing with you?

Laure Marmontel: We knew a lady who had money sleeping in her ex-company's IRA. Her plan was to buy a house and flip it, but she was too busy dealing with family matters. So she transferred her funds into a self-directed IRA so she could invest in real estate and keep the IRA tax advantages. She invested it in one of our properties and was thrilled to see the comfy returns. Gone was her guilt of missing out on real estate profits. She was taking care of herself financially while busy full time taking care of the family who meant the world to her, and that gave her peace of mind.

What inspired you to become a real estate investor?

Laure Marmontel: I was working a 9-to-5 for many years taking care of the financial matters of companies and high net worth individuals but thought there had to be more than this daily grind. Then the downturn hit. I knew that it was the right time to invest in real estate. I really struggled until I found the right real estate education and mentor. This is why I am so happy to be contributing to this book to help women succeed faster!

Can you share a lesson you learned early on as an investor that makes you a more valuable real estate investor today to work with?

Laure Marmontel: At the very beginning of our business relationship, my partner and I decided to go ahead with a small property project together, just to test our work relationship. In retrospect, it is hilarious because that deal did not correspond to any of our current acquisition criteria. It actually turned into a real pain, but we stuck it out together, and we made it. And that's when I knew that I had something solid with him.

The lesson learned: make sure that you have a strong team. Now, we do.

What's the most important question women should ask themselves as they consider where they are today, where they want to be tomorrow, and how they plan to get there?

Laure Marmontel: Determining what resources they have available is important—time, money, knowledge, energy, etc., the timeline of the real estate investment they're considering and when they'll get their capital back (24 months, 3 to 7, or more years …), how often and how much time they are willing to dedicate to review and evaluate new investment opportunities. What level of risk are they willing to accept? With higher risks sometimes come higher rewards. There are many types of real estate investments offered out there. We offer investments that we believe present an excellent mix of adjusted risk, capital preservation, and returns.

What three qualities should a woman reading your chapter consider when choosing a real estate investor to work with?

Laure Marmontel: First, track record. We mentioned it earlier, experience is very important.

Second, transparency! How much information are these real estate professionals willing to share with you before and after you invest? How available are they to answer your questions and to explain the numbers?

Third, I like the personal compatibility test as well because it's important to share the same fundamental values in life. Do they implement green energy-saving upgrades at the property? Do they care? Or do they only value money and have lost touch with the human component? Can you build a personal relationship with these people? Do you even like these people? We believe in only doing business with the people we like. We, as women, have excellent intuition, and I believe we should trust it.

Again, I'm sure you've piqued some interest in your investment opportunities. So, for a woman who might say, "I'm already earning six figures" or "This sounds good, but I don't have the bandwidth to add anything else to my plate," why should she still consider adding real estate investing to her portfolio?

Laure Marmontel: Well, investing in real estate does not have to be an active time-consuming matter. You have no idea what the CEOs of General Electric, Ford, or Apple are really working on. With our investments, the business plan is simple: upgrade the property, increase profits. We share regular information with our investors, send videos, reports, do webinars. Investors can drive by the property anytime and hug it if they want; it's there, and it's theirs. They can call us every week with questions, or they may prefer to just go deposit their cash flow checks every quarter and skip our reporting ... They can choose the level of involvement they feel comfortable with.

How can someone find out more about you and your real estate opportunities?

Laure Marmontel: Our website is www.InvestWithCip.com. I also have my own personal page called www.LaureMarmontel.com where I share productivity tips and other meaningful info. We, women, have so much to do in our busy lives. We want to get the most done in the least amount of time. I'm so grateful for living my dream, and I want to support as many as possible to reach their dreams too!

About Laure Marmontel

Company: Cornerstone Investment Partners, LLC

Who I can help: Professional women working by the hour or busy executives who are interested in making passive income through real estate and can't devote time to finding, analyzing, or managing the properties themselves.

What sets me apart:
I have worked in finance, my family business is in construction, and I understand the markets and syndication. I've experienced the same fears about investing, and I have now owned/ controlled over 1,000+ apartment units and other commercial real estate.

Testimonial: "If there is anyone who exhibits true professionalism and integrity, it would be Laure Marmontel! To say she is knowledgeable in her field is an understatement. She is as genuine as the day is long and truly cares about her clients." –D.C., TX

How to get in touch with me:
Email: Laure@InvestWithCip.com
Website: InvestWithCIP.com

Social Media:
LinkedIn.com/in/LaureMarmontel
Facebook.com/YourLaureMarmontel

Scan here to learn more:

A Woman Who Helps Urban Women 'Find the Money' to Invest in Real Estate

Are you a career woman or mother that has always wanted to pursue real estate investing but doesn't know where to start or who to work with? Would you like to find a way to invest in real estate with little to no money of your own? Lanisha Stubbs is on a mission to help Urban working moms 'find the money or use OPM (Other People's Money)' so that they can build wealth and create a passive income stream.

Whether you get one-on-one mentoring directly from Lanisha or you join her ALL women investors' club and get moral support from other hard-working and determined women who are also learning the investing ropes, you can take the necessary steps to change your current finances and start building passive income and long-term wealth.

Lanisha has been a real estate broker for over thirteen years, is also a member of the National Association of Real Estate Brokers (NAREB) and has helped facilitate hundreds of transactions.

Her specialty is teaching real estate investing to women and educating them about their finances in the process. Lanisha wants (you) women to have a seat at the table. So, if you have been considering getting into the 'Real Estate Game,' you now have your own Phil Jackson (success coach).

You will learn how you can start your own business and build wealth that will put you in a position to build generational wealth and leave a legacy that your children's children can benefit from.

Conversation with Lanisha Stubbs

Tell us about your company, what you do, and the benefit that a woman would have by working with you.

Lanisha Stubbs: My company [Wesity Real Estate Group] works with investment properties, pre-foreclosure, probate, distressed bacon, and branding properties. We work with cash investors to fix-and-flip or buy and hold rental units. Investors come in, remodel or reposition the property to increase the value, and then resell it.

I'm also the founder of the Los Angeles Women in Real Estate Group (LA WIRE), where we focus on three things: how to analyze a property; how to find private equity partners; and how to negotiate favorable terms, such as seller-financing. This is an investors' club specifically for women, which helps them learn the ropes of real estate investing as well as how to market themselves as professional investors and create REAL passive income for themselves and their families.

What specific aspects of the investing process do you help clients with?

Lanisha Stubbs: Specifically, I am an acquisition and reposition specialist. This means that I show clients how to buy and where to buy to make the highest profits. I also show my clients how to identify motivated sellers and distressed properties and then how to make an offer on them. I consult throughout the acquisition process as well as during the repositioning period to sell for the highest and best price.

I'm located in Inglewood, born and raised in South Los Angeles, and I work all of Los Angeles County real estate markets. In the South Los Angeles market, there is a significant amount of homes owned by senior citizens that are on a fixed income. So, there is deferred maintenance within the property that, unfortunately, they haven't been able to do anything about. As a Real Estate Solution Provider, I show my clients how to create win-win situation, leaving the owner and property in a better position. I show them how to create equity that everyone involved can benefit from.

So, what makes you stand out from other real estate investors or brokers in your area?

Lanisha Stubbs: I think the main thing which causes me to stand out is that I take a unique approach to my clients—by consulting first. We focus on goal setting initially, so their action plan is very intentional for accomplishing their goals.

With my clients, I focus on helping them gain a sense of confidence, as well as mastering how to analyze property, to easily identify a 'deal.' In addition, I also teach them how to speak intelligently about real estate investing, particularly when talking to private investors, as well as how to negotiate favorable terms directly with sellers.

I help my clients get past some of their challenges, mainly by helping them get past personal fears of investing. When they become equipped with the skills and knowledge to be able to properly invest, they have that behind them forever. As a result, my clients have a sense of confidence; they also have the support of the other women in the investors' club, supporting them. This allows them to go out and negotiate with a sharpened level of competence, knowing that they can come back, share the information and be confident that they are making a sensible investment.

I have a lot of experience in this arena not just from being an investor but also from being a working mom—a professional woman myself. I understand, firsthand, how challenging it is to balance your time and resources, still be present, while trying to advance the family by making smart passive income investments. And then, on top of that, being that example for your kids to do the same. So, I understand that the balance is delicate, but I also think that making passive investments is something more women should take advantage of, which will free up more time than they think. When working with me, someone that gets it, it's very feasible for them to do.

Getting over the initial fear is critical to the long-term success. Once you have done three deals, and you learn what you're doing, you will learn the transactional steps are the same for most acquisitions. That helps you gain confidence that you can negotiate any deal, help the sellers and partners and make your profits at the end of the day. It's very feasible to do; half of it is just knowing how to meet your investment goals.

Why would you say your role, particularly within the realm of acquisition, is important to the process of real estate investing?

Lanisha Stubbs: I think one of the most important things is working with someone that understands the market cycle. I play a critical role in helping clients avoid common pitfalls that a lot of new investors usually face such as buying too high or not performing their due diligence.

I also have a large database of professionals, which provides them access to the right resources that will save investors both time and money. One of the main reasons that people might hire a broker is for contract compliance. I make sure the terms in your contract match your acquisition intentions and make sure that you're never in jeopardy of losing your capital investments. So, hiring an informed broker that understands the contractual terms is very critical to the success of the negotiation.

What do you help prevent that could possibly occur during the real estate transaction?

Lanisha Stubbs: One of the most common fears with real estate investing is that of never being totally ready. We, women, tend to make sure that everything is perfect and in order before taking the first step. The reality, though, is that it's just not always perfect. We tend to wait, overthink and let the opportunity pass by—then it's just a wish and a conversation. So, a lot of times, it's getting past that initial fear. Not being afraid to make offers and fail forward.

Another common pitfall that new investors have is not having an exit strategy. So, you must ask yourself what are your desires and needs. Do you need cash flow, capital, or a better return on your savings? You should determine how long you plan to keep it or, if it's a short-term investment, where you're forcing appreciation by improving the asset and quickly reselling it. It's critical to make sure that your numbers are run for both profit and a repair budget. You also must look at all the contingencies such as permits and blueprints you might need for major restructuring projects and how that impacts your timeline. There are all kinds of pitfalls that you can fall in if you're not clear on what your exit strategy really is.

So, in relation to, kind of, DIY real estate investors, the fact that everyone feels like they can do these things for themselves and kind of be on their own, why would you tell someone that it's important to work with a real estate broker if they want to start investing and not necessarily to go about the entire process on their own?

Lanisha Stubbs: I think that a lot of TV shows have allowed the DIY industry to come into the public eye and really grow, which is wonderful. However, a lot of these shows edit out the pitfalls that can be common in real estate investments. There are a bunch of pitfalls and challenges that those DIY TV shows don't show you. They show you the ugly house, then the beautiful one, and you think that you can do that too. But it's way more involved than that, and you really want someone on your team that has experience doing this, that can guide you through the process.

That's the advantage of working with brokers that are also investors: they know this from personal experience and from representing and working on behalf of their clients. No one wants a client who walks away from the deal feeling miserable about the transaction. You want your client to feel that this was a good transaction, that they learned a lot along the way and that they want to buy more real estate in the future. That, to me, is the measure of success when working with a client.

What kind of challenges in the procurement process do you help new investors to avoid?

Lanisha Stubbs: I think the biggest advantage I give my clients is knowing the market and negotiating directly with motivated sellers. Pursuing listed properties is great; however, they are usually priced at a six percent markup for the agents' commission. I teach my clients how to identify motivated sellers, what to say when they reach out to them to negotiate favorable terms, such as seller financing. In short, this allows them to create those win-win transactions for everyone involved.

What challenges would you say investing in real estate could help or alleviate for women?

Lanisha Stubbs: I would say that one of the biggest challenges is properly investing, and knowing the market so you can successfully turn a profit. There is always a risk involved with any investment. But I would say that investing in real estate can be rewarding and can help supplement your income with passive income, which can lead to so many personal benefits.

In my opinion, the most important benefit is creating generational wealth and the legacy of passing cash flowing assets to the next generation. When I was growing up, I had all these lessons ingrained in me on how my life should be; it was a cultural thing, which led me to be taught that way. But now, working with mentors and investors, and networking outside of my community, I see real estate for what it is: an investment tool to better you and your family's lives.

The real key to financial freedom is learning how to create passive income. I think that's the biggest benefit that I'm able to show my clients, which allows them to pass these lessons onto their kids.

Can you share a success story about someone who's worked with you?

Lanisha Stubbs: I think the one that stands out the most in my career is the story of the two veterans that I was able to work with.

One day, while out with my family for popcorn, we drove down the street and saw these huge bushes in front of an old rundown property, strewn with old cars. I wrote the address down, and when we returned home, I looked it up. I found that it was a four-unit detached property, with a beautiful landscape and a great set-up. The next day, my husband and I went over to talk to the owners, only to discover two veterans living there. They lived in one of the four units, on a fixed income, with the other three units filed with old junk and in need of a lot of repairs in general.

The men did not want to sell, simply because they wanted to pass the property to their daughters. However, at this point, the only thing they would be passing down was a property tax bill because the property was not creating income for them, and they needed a significant amount of work done. Over the course of the next year, we worked with them to get on title and to get a loan to repair all the units. They were able to stay in the front unit, and we leased the other three units to tenants at market rents.

Once they were repaired, we rented them for about $1,800 per month and split the profits with them. Overall, the increase in property value went from $300,000 to $1.1million. We increased the owner's income, as well as made our intended profits, and they lived in a remodeled unit while renting the other three. We put the property in a trust, and both families benefited from the ownership. The icing on the cake was the appreciation expressed by their daughters.

I can name a bunch of different stories similar to this one, but at the end of the day, it's really our goal to create a win-win solution with real estate. There are so many opportunities, and they're just unlimited possibilities.

What would you say inspired you to become a real estate broker?

Lanisha Stubbs: I just graduated from college and got a full-time job working for a federal government agency. When I started working, I looked around the office and saw many older employees—sixty or seventy years old—that were unhappy and couldn't retire because they didn't have any resources or savings. At one point, I said, "That would never be me: only having my job, no savings and no plan to progress in life."

I decided to get my agent's license with a friend from college, and I became my own first client. I started by buying rentals in South L.A., and I used my commission to fix them up to either rent or resell them. I took a lot of my profits and started investing in newly constructed condos and lofts in Atlanta, G.A.

After my third deal, I was fearless! This was the first few years of my independent adult life, and I was having a ball. What really motivated me was just knowing that I didn't want my job to be my only source of income.

What's a lesson you learned early on that made you stronger as a broker and that you still use today?

Lanisha Stubbs: I think that my biggest lesson came during the real estate crash in 2006. At that point, I had properties all over Los Angeles and Atlanta, including new construction projects. When the market crashed, I had to be on top of the problem to ensure that I didn't get upside down in my rentals. I lost a couple of assets and learned priceless lessons.

Going through a market cycle, with its ups and downs, I think provided me with the biggest lessons overall. When I came back to L.A. after the market crash, I went back to the government job that I had and licked my wounds, but I got right back into the game. I started back by representing clients in short sales and foreclosures. See, I had the skills and the know-how to invest and having that skill ensuring me that I could do it over and over in any market situation. I now know better than I did before, and I teach that to my clients as well: acquire the skill, and you can create profits time and time again. It was in that downward market that I learned how to fish.

Essentially, now, when I work with clients, it's a passion project. I teach my clients how to find motivated sellers that are selling at a wholesale price. I teach them to know their numbers so they don't buy too high. So no matter what, they are going to make a profit.

What is something that you would tell everyone to ask themselves when they think about where they are today, where they want to be in the future, and what they should ask themselves to get there?

Lanisha Stubbs: Something that you really must ask yourself is if you are satisfied with where your life is or where it's going. The second thing to ask yourself is if you are looking for something that helps you make a difference in others' lives, in your own life, and in the lives of future generations. I think everyone should consider investing in real estate because of the sheer excitement from investing. However, I also think that the benefit of passive income is something that should be carefully considered: it will free up your lifestyle tremendously so you have more options for your time and resources.

What are three qualities someone should look for in a broker?

Lanisha Stubbs: I like to say that the three main qualities are 'The Three Es': Experience, Expertise, and Expectations.

If you want to look for a broker to work with, then you should make sure that they have the Experience and know-how to best advise you. A brand new broker who has never invested may not be the best one if you are looking to get into rental property investment versus a primary residence.

With Expertise, you should ask if the person has the expertise in real estate you are looking to invest in. If someone has never negotiated a multi-family property, you may not want to be the first one that they do it on.

The last part is that they can meet the Expectations that you set. When working with someone, you will always have certain expectations for them—a critical part of the initial consultation you should have when interviewing brokers. You want to make sure that they're able to meet the expectations that you have set and get testimonies from prior clients.

Those are the three needs that you should address when deciding on the best broker to work with.

So, for anyone who reads this book and decides, "I think investing might be good for me," what do you want them to know?

Lanisha Stubbs: If you think you can do it, then you absolutely can. A major step is finding a mentor to help you get to where you want to be and to start learning from them. Make it a habit to learn from the best until you have mastered the game yourself, then share with those new to business what you learned. In addition, work with investor-friendly brokers that are willing to take the time to grow with you and meet the 3 Es mentioned earlier.

Most importantly, don't be afraid to fail forward; get out there and talk to sellers and investors. You will be really surprised where you land.

How can someone interested get into contact with you?

Lanisha Stubbs: If you're an active investor and looking for your next investment, or new and looking for a broker/mentor, feel free to give me a call at (800) 400-8838.

About Lanisha Stubbs

Company: Wesity, Inc.

Who I can help: As a Broker, Investor and Real Estate Solution Provider, I assist urban professionals to build generational wealth and create a legacy for their family by building wealth through real estate investing.

What sets me apart: I practice what I preach. As a working mom, wife, and business owner, I understand the challenges we face with limited time, resources and knowledge to build passive income. I learned strategies that allow you to start investing, despite those barriers of entry. I also have a contribution mindset—to improve the lives of those in my community, homeowners in challenging property circumstances, and investor clients that partner with me. It's all about creating win-win solutions for all involved.

Testimonial: My club members and clients say, "I didn't know where to start before working with Lanisha and her dream team." "She showed me how it was possible to achieve my investment goals and make more time to be there for my family. I now have something to leave my kids, and more importantly, I can now teach them how to use real estate to achieve financial freedom." "I couldn't have done this without their help."

How to get in touch with me:
Email: LStubbs@WesityInc.com
Website: WesityInc.com and LawIRCClub.com

Social Media:
Facebook: Facebook.com/Wesity
Instagram: Instagram.com/lstubbsbroker
Linkedin.com: LinkedIn.com/in/larealestate

Scan here to learn more:

A Man is Not a Retirement Plan: A Smart Investment that Requires Little to No Money

'DR TAX LIEN'

Have you been hoping that your knight in shining armor would appear toting a strong financial portfolio so you will never have to worry about money again? Sorry, ladies, but situations like Meghan Markle don't happen very often; but there are smart investments that require little to no money down you can learn about and secure your own future.

Dr. Marijo Wilson offers a range of investment opportunities that can require small amounts of money (as small as $30) with a 12–36% return backed by collateral. With these numbers, can you get started investing?

Dr. Wilson wasn't always in a financially secure position. Wilson quickly realized herself that having a retirement account and making returns inside that retirement account are two different things. Building wealth a few dollars at a time can be achieved through tax liens. She is on a mission to help women become self-sufficient and create their own retirement safety net.

Dr. Marijo has compassion with clients because she knows what it was like to be a professional woman and feel burdened by the societal belief that a man is the answer to problems. She empowers women so you are in a position to choose a man because you love him and not because they can take care of you. Self-sufficiency, self-esteem, and financial independence are her three keys to a happy and successful life. This doctor has more degrees than a thermometer! Let her prescribe you a plan to build wealth through real estate investing.

Conversation with Marijo Wilson Ph.D.

Tell us about your company, your focus, and how investing in real estate can enhance, change and positively impact a woman's life.

Dr. Marijo Wilson: I specialize in tax lien and deed investments. My company is Dr. Tax Lien, Inc. Tax liens and deeds are sound investments for both women and men. Unfortunately, most people have very little or no savings at all as they approach retirement. At retirement age, it is more important to invest in low-risk strategies. At the same time, in order to increase your 'nest egg,' you need high returns. Most of us have been taught that the higher the returns, the higher the risk. Tax liens are a high return, low-risk investment strategy. We've also been taught that knowledge is power. In fact, knowledge reduces risk, and it is the application of knowledge that is power. I teach women about all the areas of real estate and help them identify the best strategies to fit their risk tolerance and lifestyle. Personally, I am particularly passionate about tax liens.

In my experience, tax liens are the perfect union inside of a retirement account. The self-directed Roth IRA allows you to create tax-free growth. You can earn twelve (12%) to thirty-six (36%) percent returns, backed by collateral. Banks and institutional investors are paying you one percent (1%) and are investing in tax liens. Learn to put your money to work for you and make the returns the banks are making. When tax liens are purchased inside the Roth IRA, you have the advantage of the high returns and tax-free growth.

Most clients believe the best part of their financial education is personal mentorship. We have a three (3) day mentorship program where we fly into your hometown. Together, we formulate a roadmap based on where you are currently positioned and where you want to go! We then begin to implement the plan by setting up the power team members in your community that will help and support you in your journey. I am available to my client to encourage, help them navigate obstacles and celebrate successes. We do individual and group coaching and have home study programs for those who cannot travel to our live training camps. We teach live training in tax liens and deeds (Tax Treasure Training), the unclaimed money business (Fund Finder Fortunes), mobile home investing (Mobile Home Millions), and general real estate investing (Real Estate Riches Unlocked).

Why is real estate investing advantageous to women?

Dr. Marijo Wilson: I believe that women have a huge advantage over men in terms of three things. Please don't tell them, though!

Women are generally more empathetic, more caring, and better listeners. Real estate is about solving challenges; it's a people business. It's not about the sticks and bricks.

What is the benefit of working with you as a tax lien and deeds expert?

Dr. Marijo Wilson: I am experienced and educated, detail oriented and structured. I provide information in a format that is both concise and easy to understand. Together, we create a plan based on multiple factors: your experience, time constraints, resources, and risk tolerance.

I've worked with hundreds of women in all fifty states. I've been teaching for over forty years, with the last fifteen in real estate. I have taught courses in tax liens and deeds since 2008. I have interviewed hundreds of tax collectors. I know the 'ins & outs' of this business and use that to help my clients. I provide you the questions to ask so that you fully understand the rules of the sale and you learn to do 'due diligence' on the properties. You should always determine which liens to add to your portfolio based on your desired outcome: are you wanting the lien to redeem and provide you with a great return on your investment (ROI) or do you want to get the deed to the property? This is the key question. Always identify your exit strategy before you buy.

What do you feel are the biggest myths when it comes to investing in real estate?

Dr. Marijo Wilson: Two come to mind immediately.

One is the myth that you must have lots of time and lots of money. Many of my clients have more money than time, and they can be pulled in a lot of different directions. It's hard to imagine adding just one more layer to an already busy schedule. But I can help with that through systems and processes which will outsource the bulk of the work. We're going to make it very systematic for them; they're going to be able to fit investing into their life when they have a strong 'why?'

The second myth is: you must become a landlord. When thinking of real estate in a traditional manner, people think about buying real estate to hold for rental income. Women hear their friends or family talk about the nightmares of dealing with tenants. Tax liens allow you to invest in real estate without the 4 Ts: Tenants, Toilets, Trash, and Termites. There are a number of real estate investment strategies where you do not have to become a landlord.

What are some common misconceptions about the real estate industry, especially since the 2008 market crash, that are not true today? And why is now a good time to invest in real estate?

Dr. Marijo Wilson: I like to say that the real estate market corrected instead of crashing. But even in 2008, there were investment opportunities. Since you can't change a market, you need to learn the existing market and then apply the correct strategies.

A real estate investment can potentially provide four (4) buckets of money: cash flow, appreciation, tax benefits (depreciation), and principal paydown. All four of these buckets are not available through other investment vehicles, and that's what makes real estate so amazing.

What are some of the most common fears that you have found that women have about getting started in real estate investing?

Dr. Marijo Wilson: I believe that the most common fear is that of losing their hard-earned reserve. Remember that there is a risk to having your money in a bank—the risk of losing your purchasing power when inflation outpaces earnings. That fear can hold people hostage, but that's why a mentor is so important. With a mentor, you can piggyback on their knowledge and experience until you're ready to move forward on your own.

How can real estate investing make a woman's life better?

Dr. Marijo Wilson: I think that real estate is very fulfilling. I believe that you get great joy from helping people and are financially rewarded at the same time. This gives you the chance to expand your influence with your additional income; this not only helps you but also your family, community, and the world.

How can you help a woman who is interested in real estate investing achieve the greatest success?

Dr. Marijo Wilson: There are many strategies in real estate investing. Some require no money or credit and a lot of time. Other strategies require very little time and require capital. No matter where you are on this continuum, you can get started and be successful. Everything you do and achieve will start with the right mindset. Invest in a top-notch mentor and get the proper training to help you select the right strategies—based on personal demands and market conditions.

Can you share a story about one of your investors and a success that they accomplished while investing with you?

Dr. Marijo Wilson: Well, that's an easy one. My standout protégé is Chimene Van Gundy, known to her followers as the 'Queen of

Mobile Homes.' When I mentored her, I asked for her permission to mentor her. She agreed to do "what I say, when I say, NO DEBATE." Part of her tremendous success is that she was very hungry. She had been abused in the corporate world and was ready to take control of her life. She was willing to do whatever it took to make that happen. In order words, she was 'coachable.' She applied what I taught her, embedded it into her DNA and now teaches others. She is living a life of passion and purpose and is paying it forward to other women.

What inspired you to become a real estate investor, and why tax liens and deeds?

Dr. Marijo Wilson: My mom and dad invested in real estate and are my inspiration. I first became aware of tax liens back in the mid-1970s. I wish that I could tell you that I immediately jumped in and started investing. As a 20-year-old, I wasn't looking for investment opportunities. I was still operating under the belief system: "Get a good education and a good job." Once I completed my doctorate degree and landed my first job as an assistant professor at the University of Kentucky, I realized I didn't really want 'a job.' After five years, I left the university and started a business. At that time, I started investing in real estate and eventually started studying and learning more about tax liens. Today, tax liens remain a very hidden area of real estate investing.

Once I had begun to apply my knowledge of tax lien investing, I quickly appreciated the benefits of this amazing strategy. I envisioned establishing a training company to help others build their wealth. My passion is to teach others, and my gift is the ability to 'break down' complicated concepts and make them easy to understand. Tax lien investing can help individuals build a portfolio of properties or obtain amazing returns on their investment dollars with minimal risk. When I'm working with a client, I walk them through all the steps: learning the strategy thoroughly, learning how to implement it themselves, and then 'paying it forward' by teaching others.

Can you share a lesson you learned early on as an investor that makes you a more valuable real estate investor today to work with?

Dr. Marijo Wilson: I like to say that if a real estate investor tells you that they've never made a bad investment, they probably haven't made an investment. I think that we've all had one or more bad experiences in our past.

As I look back on my investment career, I realize that the one-percent rule would have helped me had I known it sooner. When I started real estate investing, I was purchasing properties without any kind of training. I just did what my parents were doing. But I didn't know how to evaluate the properties for cash flow. I was buying properties and renting them out but didn't know the 'One Percent Rule' (1% Rule). For an investment property to have positive cash flow with minimal down payment, you should be able to get monthly rents greater than or equal to one percent of the purchase price. I wasn't buying properties at the right price point to make this work, so I was working to support my properties. Your properties should always be supporting you when working with real estate investments—not the other way around.

What's the most important question women should ask themselves as they consider where they are today, where they want to be tomorrow, and how they plan to get there?

Dr. Marijo Wilson: I encourage my clients to thoroughly evaluate their reasons for investing. They should ask themselves 'why?' "Why would I want to do this?" When you have a strong 'why,' the other answers will fall into place. Your 'why' can be like the seatbelt on a roller coaster. If you don't buckle your seatbelt, you will be thrown off the rollercoaster of life. If you don't have a strong 'why,' you will give up when times get tough. Your 'why' is what keeps you firmly in your seat, moving forward through all the ups and downs life throws at you.

Additionally, everyone needs to take an inventory of their time. Time is the one commodity that you can't make more of. Our clients must ask themselves if they are willing to sacrifice to create a richer life for their family in the future. I've found that when they have a strong 'why,' they will find the time.

What three qualities should a woman reading your chapter consider when choosing a real estate investor to work with?

Dr. Marijo Wilson: There are five factors to look for when choosing a mentor for real estate investing: Above board, Active investor, Articulate, Accessible, and Applaud your successes.

The person you're working with should be above board. They should be honest, straightforward and frank. I think that you've got to find someone who's not afraid to say what you need to hear. There are ways to say these things without being rude. This person needs to have a good 'bedside manner'—one who isn't abrupt and abrasive.

Secondly, your mentor should be an active investor. They should be experienced. This is the most important part when you are looking for someone to teach you—they need the experience to back up their knowledge.

Thirdly, they need to be articulate. There are going to be lots of processes and procedures that are new to you. Your mentor should be able to explain all concepts in a logical step-by-step manner that is easy to understand. This way, you can gain the confidence in your understanding and can move forward with the implementation of your strategy.

The fourth point is accessibility. You want to work with someone that is responsive. In this business, you will need to be able to reach them if you are having trouble. You shouldn't have to jump through hoops to get to them and should be able to get in touch with no fuss.

And lastly, it's important to work with someone that will applaud your successes with you. As I mentioned before, I always celebrate successes with my clients, and I think this is important, especially to women. I've noticed that many times women don't get positive affirmations. People aren't giving us the affirmations we all need to feel good about ourselves. I suggest my clients get in front of a mirror and give themselves the positive affirmations they need to hear. Tell yourself that you're fantastic, you're smart, you're intelligent, and you can do it. Tell yourself whatever works for you. When you have started to change your mind, everything will change—your thoughts, your world, your life. Every single change in your life will start with your thoughts.

I'm sure you've piqued some interest in your investment opportunities. So, for a woman who might say, "I'm already earning six figures," or for a woman who might already have too much on her plate, why should she still consider adding real estate investing to her portfolio?

Dr. Marijo Wilson: I went to college for twelve years, became a professor and had a revelation five years later: I was never going to get ahead working for someone else. So, I quit my position and started my own business.

I think even if you love your profession, you should have a backup plan. According to the Harvard Business Review, 41% of women working in tech eventually leave the field. Women are also reaching retirement age with very little savings. So, everyone should have both a 'Plan A' (your job) and a 'Plan B' (secondary income streams). When you work for someone else, you don't have the same security that you can create when building something for yourself. It takes a lot more time, and you must work more hours, but in the end, this is something that is your very own!

Keep in mind, too, that most people will think that they are earning enough money, while they are working themselves to death. At that point, you are exchanging your hours for dollars. Time is a commodity that you can't get back, as I mentioned before. So, if you think that you don't have the time, or you have plenty of money, then you won't be working for yourself; you will still be exchanging your hours for dollars. The way that you break this cycle comes from Warren Buffett: "If you don't find a way to make money while you sleep, you will work until you die." When you work for yourself, you will make money while you sleep, and have dollars working for dollars, without exchanging your precious time for it.

How can someone find out more about you and your real estate opportunities?

Dr. Marijo Wilson: They can find me through my website: www.DrTaxLien.com. If you are interested in setting up a consultation, you can email me directly at marijo@drtaxlien.com.

Marijo Wilson Ph.D.

Company: Dr. Tax Lien, Inc.

Who I can help: Women just getting started with investing; women that want a higher return on their investments; women that need to build their retirement savings; women who have a strong 'why' to do something extraordinary; women who want financial independence; women looking for a 'Plan B.'

What sets me apart: I am highly educated and have years of teaching experience. I am a seasoned investor and practice what I preach. I am passionate about helping others fulfill their destiny.

Testimonial: "Dr. Marijo has completely changed my life. Her teachings took me from a negative net worth to the Mobile Home Millionaire. Her positivity and passion propelled me to be an authority in my niche. I know she can do the same for you too." –Chimene Van Gundy

How to get in touch with me:
Email: marijo@drtaxlien.com
Website: www.drtaxlien.com

Social Media:
Facebook: Marijo Wilson and Dr Tax Lien
Twitter: drmarijo and drtaxlien
LinkedIn: LinkedIn.com/in/marijowilson-drtaxlien
Instagram: drmarijowilson
Google+: Dr Marijo Wilson
Pinterest: Dr Tax Lien Pinterest.com/drmarijow

Scan here to learn more:

Stop the Phone from Ringing: Automate the Management of Your Properties

Are you looking for a way to manage your properties in a more organized way? Are you tired of middle-of-the-night phone calls or would you like a system that keeps your paperwork and team organized so you don't have to? Linda Liberatore has been providing automated support systems for landlords that own two or more properties for over 20 years. Her success has led her to speak around the country to landlords as a leader in property management and the real estate industry.

Linda wasn't always such a self-sufficient woman, and her story is like many of ours. She began as a first-time homebuyer who found her passion in real estate and dreamed of making a career out of it. That passion led Linda to create a property management business, called My Landlord Helper, that acts to bridge the gap that tends to form between first-time investors and their tenants. Linda helps landlords not feel threatened by technology and offers resources and automation that make property management simple and streamlined so you can use your time on the things you want to. Find out how to go from frustrated landlord managing a few properties to the tech-savvy investor that can manage even more properties and still have full control.

Conversation with Linda Liberatore

What do you do and how do you help real estate investors?

Linda Liberatore: Certainly. I own a property management company called My Landlord Helper. We take the headache out of landlording for investors. We now also have an app tied to our company that offers a lot of do-it-yourself information.

When you get into real estate, you don't think about the minute tasks that you have to deal with daily. You will have things that need to be done, such as keeping up with lease renewals, but you will have smaller things, such as legal notices, that can get lost in the shuffle. These are small details, but they are significant. Often, many new do-it-yourself realtors that I have worked with have been bogged down by these problems just because they do tend to pile up quickly and can get them into trouble.

Really, mostly what I do is just management. What I call it, mainly, is interfacing with the tenants. Ultimately, we are on the road to becoming the face of the real estate owners to the tenants. We operate the software, document everything, work with anyone—from lawyers to maintenance. We prepare legal documents and are even accountants. At the core, I like to use the analogy that we are the hub, and our clients are the spokes in the wheel of the company itself. We relay the information to the higher-ups from the spoke but will also make sure that everything runs smoothly.

What would you say are the advantages of starting a real estate business for women that currently have a job?

Linda Liberatore: I would like to go back to the analogy of the hub for this question. So, the analogy of the hub and the spoke; let's go to the wheel. Now, a wheel doesn't move unless someone causes it to, right? Well, I would say that's like us. Any of our clients would tell you that they are moving forward in their business because of what we're doing. We coordinate simple things, and it takes a lot of pressure off them.

There are a lot of benefits to having a job like this. The best is having your own hours, which is important to me, personally, as a mom. When I started this business, I was looking for part-time work, being a mom. Now, though, I have passive income and the flexible hours I need. It does take hard work, but this kind of work can create a sizable passive income.

What are the biggest myths out there when it comes to transitioning from a job to owning a business?

Linda Liberatore: I think one of the biggest myths is that you don't have to outsource, that you can do everything yourself. That is so wrong, though, because you should be working with other companies. You all should be working together as a team, and part of that is outsourcing things to others that can help you.

What would you say are some common misconceptions women have about hiring a manager to help them manage their properties?

Linda Liberatore: I always say that getting a real estate manager to help run your property is like doing your tax returns. You might think that there is no reason you can't do this yourself, you should just get Turbo Tax or something. You'll be fine, right?

Well, you might think that you can get in there and get it done, but you will end up running into a lot of grey areas. Since you aren't totally sure of the answer, you err on the part of the fear that you have. You think that you should be more conservative here and not get back as much as you should have. But if you have a professional there, helping you, they know how to run a business and not get into trouble, which can clarify a lot of those grey areas. This can also help you get back all the money that you need.

What are some of the most common fears that you've specifically heard women express about managing properties? And what can you and your company do to help them get past these fears?

Linda Liberatore: I really would say that women feel fear of the unknown. This makes them worry about their first move and tends to hold them back.

So, there are different levels of investors, which can change what they fear. Mostly, I've dealt with smaller investors: either those that don't have much money invested or they have just gotten started. One of the biggest challenges at this level is the fear of the unknown. You know, there are a lot of managers that aren't sure what legal document goes with which situation—you know, things like that. So, these investors are uncertain, especially when they realize that they are dealing with people's lives, their homes. You must know what you are doing, which can be scary.

I think even after these investors have been established, they are still scared. They aren't prepared for certain things: uncomfortable situations, such as rent; unnecessary expenses; fees for legal expenses. These are not things that anyone expects going in on the ground floor.

I think that the best way to get these women past their fears is to have them believe in themselves. Don't act too quickly, don't be too impulsive, but always believe in yourself. Trust and verify first, always.

I would say, first off, empower yourself with knowledge. Find the experts in the other chapters and pick out ones that would likely help you make your first move. Acquire your property—believe me, it's out there. I believe that I've been in over ten different real estate investment groups, both nationwide and locally. I think that this plays into getting knowledge, and always be learning.

This comes to hard work and who you surround yourself with as well. Back, many years ago, Les Brown's motivational tape came out. One of his stories was about how there was somebody in his life that was very, very wealthy. He said he would go into this person's office to shine shoes, and while doing so, he listened to how the businessman talked on the phone and learned so much through him. I would say that the same could be said of the woman that thinks she can't do it. Like, she should go to the meetings, absorb, find a guru. Find the successful people in the group and find out what you can do for them.

The last thing is to always act on your plan. All too often, you learn and learn but then don't go and do it. The easiest way to do this is not to be alone. So, go find the person that you would trust as a partner. Make sure that there is a huge mutual trust with this person, and then start your partnership from there!

Real estate now is nothing but an increase. Sure, we have downturns, but if you set aside an affordable amount and not think that you are going into this as a fix-and-flipper, you will be fine. This brings in a lot of cash flow if you work it.

I think that the other thing I'd say is that it's always going to come back to hard work. I don't care if it's Jennifer Lopez or LeBron James; they are going to tell you that it's not all glamour, not all lights—it's lots of hours behind the scenes, and if you're committed, you can do it.

What are some common pitfalls that women tend to have when they have to manage their first properties?

Linda Liberatore: I think that sometimes people don't understand that while we are a company, we are also a team.

I think a lot of investors, as well, are afraid to outsource. This can have a real advantage because you're paying a company, not a worker. If this company is no good, you can just let them go without any of the drama that can be associated with firing a worker. This makes a much easier transition period and makes everything run smoothly.

What inspired you to become a coach for women?

Linda Liberatore: I like to think that one of these things is totally accidental. I have three daughters, and I think because of that, I've mostly hired women.

I do feel like going through the boot camp—which is what I call my office—really does empower these young ladies. I don't have a degree in technology; I have a passion for it—I just love it. So, in hiring these women, I'm passing that passion on and showing that you don't have to have a degree to follow your love. We cross-train all our employees, as well, to get them used to doing different tasks in this environment; so, I feel like that really empowers them as well. They know that they can go out and get any job because they have done everything in this environment.

What inspired you to become a property manager?

Linda Liberatore: I have a unique story, I think.

I needed a part-time job that worked with me being a mom. I had already worked on technology and always did a lot of technology training. I had also worked extensively as a bookkeeper. After I started working with this, I would introduce these property managers to software that fits their needs, along with things like Quick Books.

Generally, I just love technology. I could see a need for what I was doing, and I felt that it was an under-served market. The do-it-yourself landlord didn't have many options. You must keep in mind that this was back when you had to have servers. Then you had to install the servers. This was time-consuming and expensive, so I thought that I could help.

Can you share a lesson that you learned early on that still affects how you do business today?

Linda Liberatore: I would like to say that this is an important lesson for anyone out there. Early on in my career, I was at this big symposium conference in Chicago for the housing community. While

I was there, I met an investor who was really struggling with this tenant. While I talked to him, I realized he had made a fundamental mistake: he let the tenant into the property before it was fully rehabilitated. Well, since he was new to this, he forgot something that you have to remember: you must document the process. So, when he came to talk to me, he was already in deep with this tenant: non-payment, etc. Well, this whole process really gave me more perspective on how I should be dealing with this and made me realize that sometimes the most important piece is knowing when to get legal help. It can be difficult early on, especially because everyone won't be able to pay for a lawyer, but it is imperative.

So, I think that my foolish mistake was almost having too big of a heart and thinking that I could help. I've learned sometimes that you can't do everything yourself, and you might have to get someone else to help you. I've learned to make a better assessment and be more confident in it as well.

What are the most important questions women should ask themselves if they are thinking of starting a business?

Linda Liberatore: When I was just starting out, I had to learn a lot of hard lessons along the way. But I've also learned how to make a better assessment and be more confident in my assessment. Early in the process, you are insecure about your own advice. I realize now that I should have trusted my advice, but, of course, experience helps with this.

What questions should women ask when they are seeking a property manager to work with?

Linda Liberatore: Well, that is a timely question!

I recently saw a quote that sums up the first two qualities to me: "To give the best service, you must add something which cannot be bought or measured with money; and that is sincerity and integrity."

Since that's only two qualities, though, I will add a third that I am personally known for: productivity. So, that's sincerity, integrity, and productivity.

So, as far as integrity, well, that's easy to measure, right? Since integrity is more a numbers-based system, then it is easy to judge within a company. Talk to the manager, look around, ask how many properties they have, how long have they been with clients—things like that. These things seem small but can be super, super important. Personally, I would want to speak to some of their existing clients. If someone that you are working with hasn't had a client in six months—well, that would be a bit of a red flag.

Productivity is a personal thing, but it is important to me. I've always just learned to say more with less. Keep in mind that if you are just starting out, you can't afford the super bloated property management companies. These might look great, but those bells and whistles come at a price. You're just going to have to get by with the do-it-yourself version of the explicit job. You need to always make the best use of your dollars when starting out.

Sincerity will come in more on how you interact with your property managers. You're putting a lot of money into someone else's hands just to not answer the phone. It's worth a little bit of time to just get onto the phone and talk with the person that you're working with, just to make sure that they are going to care about your needs.

Can you share a success story of a woman that you helped?

Linda Liberatore: So, I slightly touched on this earlier, but I'll go into more detail. A man, a client, came to us; he was in a space situation. When he came to us, he probably had almost a hundred units. He was in a bind because one of his workers essentially just walked off the job. This place didn't have any cross-training in place, so no one else in the office knew what was going on. Like, there's a software solution, but there's nothing that's entered because no one else knows how to put it in. And then when we started to untangle the problem, the reason that she had left so unexpectedly is, there was a lot of missing money.

You must also remember that while we are trying to fix this, we are live—we have people trying to pay rent, people calling in problems. We literally have a desk right out front of that office with no one sitting there. So, we had to bring on specifically ten people to help with the fire because we had calls that were going undocumented; so, one of the first things that we had to do is make sure that the calls get into the system. Then we had to help him allocate his resources and see who was paying or not paying.

It was a remarkable turn-around how we got them on course and data, ledgers updated, and so many other things. We had an experienced staff to be able to put together quickly and easily where he had just gone out and hired somebody. It was scary, and I had to offer lots of incentives for my own team to want to answer those calls—especially since they hadn't been attended to for a bit.

What would you leave women with that are thinking of starting a new business or have started a new business and are struggling?

Linda Liberatore: I would really say the one thing that holds people back is going beyond the fear. Like, really believing in yourself. Don't act too quickly, because you don't want to be impulsive, but be a go-get-them type of person. You can do that, but we will do that. And again, trust and verify. I think those are the most important things.

How can someone that is interested in working with you get into contact with you?

Linda Liberatore: I would love to have everyone subscribe to my YouTube Channel, SECUREPAYONE. We have over 600 videos, free webinars, and software interviews; all of these are great solutions for the do-it-yourself landlord.

About Linda Liberatore

Company: My Landlord Helper

Who I can help: I love to work with DIY landlords of any size. Landlords that have a clear set of goals to grow their portfolio. I know I can assist them in achieving their vision.

What sets me apart: I have a unique partnership with my clients that enables me to ask a series of questions that are focused on the client's goals. I have a heart in each of these business relationships. My clients know that our process is transparent and is 200% committed to their success.

Testimonial: "My Landlord Helper's systems and solutions have helped me free up my time to make more deals and acquire more properties. SPO processes have assured the back end is always taken care of. We focus on acquisition and rehab while My Landlord Helper is assisting us with achieving key business objectives with our buy and hold."

How to get in touch with me:
Website: MyLandlordHelper.com
Linked In: Linda Liberatore

Social Media:
YouTube: YouTube.com/securepayone
Facebook: Facebook.com/mylandlordhelper

Scan here to learn more:

U.S. Income-Generating Investments!

Do you believe it's difficult to create wealth through real estate investing? Are you a non-U.S. person interested in investing in the U.S. but without any idea where to start or who you can trust to work with? Daniella and Kevin Dhillon are just the partners you need. Both of them were born in Malaysia and raised in Australia; they specialize in working with overseas investors and understand the fears and concerns of prospective non-U.S. people interested in investing in the U.S. The Dhillons have been investing in real estate since 2006.

Daniella and Kevin also work with many U.S. investors as well. This dynamic duo has learned how to crush it in both the Australian and U.S. real estate markets and are committed to helping overseas investors become successful in U.S. real estate investing. They have walked in the shoes and know the reservations overseas people have about investing in the U.S., like not being able to see the properties in person and not wanting to get scammed. Because the U.S. is a completely different country, there are a lot of unknown risks, but Daniella and her husband have the experience and success to help navigate you through the process.

Whether you have large savings, a 401(k), or just want to learn how to get started, Daniella and Kevin can help you find U.S. real estate investments that are income-generating.

Conversation with Daniella Dhillon

Tell us about your company, your focus, and how investing in real estate can enhance, change and positively impact a female or non-U.S. resident's life.

Daniella Dhillon: My husband Kevin and I are the founders of Dhillon Partners, a company that offers unique solutions to U.S. real estate ownership. We take care of the headaches that can come part and parcel with landlord ownership.

Our company runs with a focus on cultivating an ongoing partnership and relationship, building our wealth together. We aren't just a company that will sell you a product and disappear; we invest our own money into each and every transaction, making us co-owners and partners in the truest sense of the word. With this better alignment of interests, we give our investors peace of mind about their properties as well as regular cash flow.

We also specialize in helping non-U.S. residents invest in real estate opportunities in the U.S. so you can take advantage of the cash flow and strong private property rights that U.S. real estate typically offers. The beauty of real estate is that it is a level playing field—it does not discriminate whether you're male or female, and in the U.S, it doesn't matter if you're not a U.S. citizen—you can still own real estate and amass a substantial portfolio for yourself.

What type of investment opportunities do you offer, and how much is required for an initial investment?

Daniella Dhillon: Typically, we select projects that fit three criteria: properties that cash-flow from day 1, landlord-friendly governance, and economically dynamic markets. This ensures investments in areas that have a growing population—generating greater capital appreciation and reducing our risk, especially in an economic downturn.

We focus on the major commercial property types—office, industrial, retail, and multifamily—with a very keen interest in the latter two. We generally shy away from residential houses. Why? Scale! It is cheaper to buy in bulk than in smaller quantities. This way, we help unlock deals and financing the average investor largely finds inaccessible. Within these categories, our company generally looks for stable, established commercial investments. One benefit of this is that it will be immediately cash-flowing from the beginning, which allows our partners and us to de-risk significantly. It also means that there is an added value for increased returns through simple means. We most often look for projects in good condition but also take on projects with simple cosmetic fixes.

Ideally, our investor would have idle capital and want to make productive use of it. Our main goal, in this vein, is giving our investors the proactive steps to set up their and their family's financial well-being.

The initial investment varies, depending on the life of the project and what type of asset we acquire.

Why do you think that investing in real estate is a wise investment or something that investors outside of the United States should do as well?

Daniella Dhillon: The majority of what my company does is called 'cash flow investing.' I'm going to borrow a quote from Grant Cardone here: "If you're not cash flowing, you're gambling." I think that investing for capital gains is another form of gambling because you are making assumptions about the future; assumptions that may or may not come true. The United States has an abundance of cash-flowing real estate assets available on the market today.

So, investing in the United States is a great idea, why?

Well, I personally think that you would be hard-pressed to find this kind of cash flow anywhere else in the world. You have an advantage of having income as well as risk mitigation in the case of a changing economic environment. We never want to be in a position where we are forced to sell. That, in my opinion, is where a lot of real estate investors become undone. Another major difference between U.S. investments and other international opportunities is strong governance and sovereign risk. Private property rights have always been strong in the U.S. because of their national philosophy of freedom and the rights of the individual. In other societies, we see this may not be the case, as nationalization is more prevalent.

With such strong fundamentals, I think that it would be challenging for you to find these same kinds of benefits anywhere else, which is why I truly believe that U.S. commercial real estate is the best investment in the world in this day and age.

Why is investing in real estate advantageous to women?

Daniella Dhillon: Real estate affords many advantages. Time is a huge factor for me. As a mother of young children, I relish and guard my time with my children. I don't want to miss out on watching them grow and develop and become more powerful each day. At this stage, 'Mommy' is still the favorite, so I count myself blessed that I can be truly present and spend as much time with them as I'd like while not having to worry about providing financially for their immediate and future needs. There is also no glass ceiling in real estate as a career. There are no legal or social rules, as assets are held in companies, so no one even thinks to question, "Is this a male or female owner?" It shouldn't matter anyway, but let's be honest—for some careers, it sadly does. Lastly, women have been in real estate for a long time. Though an allegory, I personally look up to the woman described in Proverbs 31 in the Bible, which was written thousands of years ago. Amongst many other things she does, verse 16 says, "She considers a field and buys it; out of her earnings she plants a vineyard." If she can do it, so can we!

What are the benefits of working with you as an investor?

Daniella Dhillon: I believe that there are multiple reasons why our company stands above the rest. The first is that we are investing our own money along with yours. The second is that we see this as an opportunity to cultivate an ongoing partnership and relationship, as we build our wealth together. Having personally resided in the U.S., we have built a great team of experts as your boots on the ground. Having an understanding of international investments and opportunity costs, we are able to provide a proven successful way into this investment class which we open to other like-minded investors.

What do you feel are the biggest myths when it comes to investing in U.S. real estate internationally?

Daniella Dhillon: A reservation one may have when investing internationally is the management of assets from a distance. There is always a fear that the property deteriorates due to mismanagement. Most times, though, we are the largest stakeholder in investments; this means that both the management and performance will personally affect us, aligning our personal interests with our investors'.

I also think that another big myth is that the American market is highly litigious and full of people that don't have your best interest at heart. There are always going to be those kinds of people in any large market. To use a metaphor, in the big wide ocean, you may be swimming with sharks, which is why you need to figure out how to be a strong swimmer and not look like bait—by getting the best team of experts around you! But I'd rather live in the ocean than a goldfish bowl! It's a matter of your own personal risk tolerance or, conversely, how ambitious, adventurous and affluent you want to be.

A final myth is that you must do this by yourself. That's not true. Being a team player is one of the secret ingredients in gaining success in real estate. I like to say that real estate is a team sport, and put simply, the best team wins. As you can see in this very book, there are so many people you can and should engage with, who bring their unique expertise to the table. As a spiritual principle, everything great in this world is made by a team of individuals. That's the essence of relationships, and real estate certainly is a relationship-driven industry.

What are some common misconceptions about the real estate industry, especially since the 2008 market crash, that are not true today? And why is now a good time to invest in real estate?

Daniella Dhillon: There are two major factors to address here: the U.S. dollar and economic dynamism.

There is a huge debt here in the U.S., that's true. And we are essentially using the weight of that debt to enrich our investors and us. Why? Which asset class is the best hedge against inflation? Real estate. The U.S. government's debt guarantees inflation is built into our economic system. Unfortunately, those earning a fixed wage will get hurt in this state of affairs, as seen in the shrinking middle class in all first world countries. The best way to protect our families, then, is to adopt a strategy that will see us survive and thrive, and we believe our approach to commercial real estate investment allows us to do just that. In today's world, adaptability is key.

Which brings me to my second point—economic dynamism. The United States is a large and turbulent market. As investors, we should not fear volatility but embrace it, especially in a market the size of the U.S. There are fifty states in the U.S., and within all these states, there are multiple markets. Put simply, you are spoilt for choice. You can find cities in areas where people are moving elsewhere, and the population is going down, and you can also find cities in areas experiencing healthy and exponential growth in jobs, even thru an economic downturn. The great thing about the U.S. is that you can find this demographic data easily. You can identify where people and jobs are moving with simple desk-based research. We do our research beforehand, which is why our investment criteria mitigate a lot of this risk: we only invest in areas with job growth, low crime, and a great appetite for the type of housing or retail product that we are offering in that market.

On a macro scale, though, we've discovered that among the major Western democracies around the world, the U.S. has the strongest demographic fundamentals when it comes to population growth—both from birth and migration. People need a place to live, to work, and to do commerce, which is why our industry is an evergreen. We are all intrinsically consumers of real estate—it's humanity's unavoidable asset class.

What are some of the most common fears that women have about getting started in real estate investing?

Daniella Dhillon: Most women I know are perfectionists. We want to get it right the first time and have everything looking beautiful and perfect. Consequently, the fear of failure or making a mistake cripples some women into inaction. However, I quote *The Art of War* by Sun Tzu, "If you set a fully equipped army in march in order to snatch an advantage, the chances are that you will be too late." Sometimes in life, you can't be 100% prepared and have all the answers or all your ducks lined up neatly in a row. Uncertainty and risk are inherent in every decision we make in life; even indecision itself bears some risks. The great thing about commercial real estate is the amount of control you have as an owner to change the outcome of how the asset performs. Values are based on Net Operating Income (NOI) as well as cap rates. Put simply, if you can problem-solve how to increase income and/or decrease expenses, you don't have to fear your imagined worst-case scenario—because you can change it. Power is the ability to do or act. Empower yourself; do something about it, about your situation. "Make it work!"

How can real estate investing make life better?

Daniella Dhillon: I think that the best part of real estate investing is the stability that people find in it. Real estate, being a tangible asset, holds intrinsic value. Land, in and of itself, is scarce because it's limited and will therefore always remain valuable to someone. We see this common view of valuation even in the ability to finance real estate-backed investments. Given this security, my investors and I always get a good night's sleep and never have to worry if we can continue to afford to maintain our standard of living. Peace of mind is priceless and surely makes for a better quality of life.

How can you help a female non-U.S. resident who is interested in finding investment opportunities in the U.S. achieve success?

Daniella Dhillon: I can certainly share my own experiences of what I have done, recommend some great books and resources, or you can leverage my knowledge and years of experience by partnering with me in my next project and actually do something about what you want! Just reach out and let's start a conversation.

Can you share a story about one of your investors and a success they accomplished while working with you?

Daniella Dhillon: The first people that came to mind are a lovely husband and wife couple from Malaysia, who are in the retirement phase of their lives. Like so many hardworking individuals, they had a healthy savings account but not much to show for it in their retirement accounts. It was the usual things: projections on their retirement funds fell short, but they still had to pay bills without their normal nine-to-five jobs. Somehow, though, it meant that they had to watch their expenses very carefully and minimize their options.

So, initially, they were resistant to investing with us internationally for all the reasons I mentioned before: being international, not knowing where the U.S. dollar was going ... etc. But we built up a good business relationship over the years—and with that, trust was gained. They decided to invest with us in one project. Then they invested with us again on another project and then another. With each new project, they were able to witness and enjoy the benefits of having an extra income stream to see that their capital was working for them.

What inspired you to become a real estate investor, and why are your investments attached to both profit and purpose?

Daniella Dhillon: The inspiration to invest in real estate began as a way to find financial freedom and support our parents financially. Admittedly, my business partner and husband, Kevin Dhillon, is the visionary in our company. He has shared our beginnings in various podcast interviews which are freely accessible and available online.

After reading numerous books, attending conferences and joining real estate investment clubs, the truth is, it only really made sense to me after we took action and actually bought our first investment property in 2006. With that property, we made more money from the cash flow and equity growth in one year than my annual starter wage. From that moment, we began acquiring as many properties as we could. It was personally challenging as young adults at the time. Instead of traveling the world or going to fancy restaurants or getting the latest fashions, we pushed every spare dollar we had into real estate and looked upon it as forced savings.

The wonderful thing about real estate is that it's not rocket science—it's simple, not a big secret, and anyone can do it. It's relatively straightforward. What we did was just replicate the same process of purchasing real estate with good value and then just rent them out. But don't misunderstand; it's simple but not easy. There is work involved, especially in the beginning. But if you stick through the process, the reward is well worth the price you pay.

With that, there are many reasons why we like to help others benefit from real estate. I have an abundance mindset and believe there is an abundance of real estate investment opportunities for every single person in this world! This is NOT a zero-sum game because value can be created, and subsequently, our creativity is limitless. Together, we can do more good! I particularly like real estate because it's a win-win, feel-good business where you are not only enjoying great returns for you and your investors, but you are creating more value, be it restoring, remodeling, or re-tenanting a vacant space. We benefit society by providing housing and places of business for the community. So, a lot of the value we achieve is through implementing strategic business plans to improve or enhance community or centers that might have been mismanaged, neglected, or just need a little bit of extra TLC.

Can you share a lesson that you learned early on as an investor that makes you a more valuable real estate investor to work with today?

Daniella Dhillon: A lesson I learned in being a real estate owner is how to pivot and respond to changing conditions. What worked yesterday might not be the most effective strategy today. This can only be learned over time through experience. Being in the business since 2006, we have had to reinvent ourselves several times since then. The good news is that long-term real estate investing can be very forgiving. Real estate is a great way to hedge against inflation.

Being flexible and open to new ideas means I stay learning, I stay hungry, and I make sure to get great mentors who are a few steps ahead of me. After all, the best mistakes to learn from are the mistakes that other people have already made.

What is the most important question that women should ask themselves as they consider where they are today, where they want to be tomorrow, and how they plan to get there?

Daniella Dhillon: Ask yourself what you are and aren't willing to pay because your dreams will always cost you something. Everyone hates buyer's remorse, and in pursuing your dreams, it's not as easy as returning that cocktail dress that you got on an impulse buy! Building your dreams takes time, and you can't get that time back—there's no refund. You don't want to find yourself 10 years from now being no closer to your goals or achieving your goals but at the cost of significant relationships or at the cost of your own personal ethics and reputation. Again, a thought-provoking quote I like from Jim Rohn is, "If the decision costs something, accept the pain but not the guilt, especially if it affects your family." In other words, count the cost.

What three qualities should a female non-U.S. resident reading your chapter consider when choosing a real estate investor to work with?

Daniella Dhillon: I think it's important for you to build trust with anyone you work with, as I certainly only work with people I trust myself. Trust can be built and is a combination of both character and competency. I personally look for those who: #1 can show a proven track record in what they do, i.e., they have good experience and success in their field; #2 are accessible and easy to work with, as open, honest communication fosters transparency; and perhaps the best is #3 what others say about them. You can always toot your own horn, but what's the verdict on the street?

I'm sure you've piqued some interest in your investment opportunities. So, for a woman who might say, "I'm already earning six figures," or who says, "This sounds good, but I don't have the bandwidth to add anything else to my plate," why should she still consider adding real estate investing to her portfolio?

Daniella Dhillon: I currently have investors who are already earning well in jobs they love. They partner with me to make their savings work hard for them. So, I would ask you, "How are your current investments working out so far, and are you happy with them?" "If there was a way in which you could achieve better returns in a shorter amount of time, is there any reason why you won't do it?" Their cash-flowing real estate investments are simply an added income stream to their lifestyles. I also currently have investors who are too busy to do what I do in real estate. The great thing about investments is that you can leverage your time by investing in other people's projects. Most people heavily rely on their jobs as their sole source of income, but sooner or later, our job careers will end; so, it's only prudent to start planning now for that day.

I think that each of us has our own personal wealth creation journey. Certainly, U.S. commercial real estate investing is not for everyone. Each of us has our own appetite for risk and reward, which may differ greatly. If you are truly happy and content with your current financial situation, then I wish you all the best and hope that this book adds some sort of entertainment value to you. But if you picked up this book because you're looking to INCREASE your wealth and change your life, then ask yourself WHY you are doing what you're doing in the first place. Your motivation will drive you to application and compel you to achieve your dreams. The key is to take MASSIVE ACTION.

How can someone find out more about you and your real estate opportunities?

Daniella Dhillon: The best way would be by going through my website: dhillonpartners.com. If you're interested in projects and would like to see if we are a good fit for you, then I invite you to apply for a complimentary 45-minute appointment with me through the calendar link on the website. You can also get ahold of me through Facebook and LinkedIn.

I host quite a few meet-ups from all around the world as well. So, we have one in Houston (Texas, United States), Hong Kong,

Singapore, Kuala Lumpur (Malaysia), and Melbourne (Australia). If you want to reach out to me, and you mention that you found out about me through reading this book, then I'll be able to send you a free resource on how to get started in real estate investing. Just ask me for my bonus 'Time Leverage Program.'

About Daniella Dhillon

Company: Dhillon Partners

Who I can help: My area of expertise is helping people to increase their savings by investing in cash-flowing U.S. real estate assets. I typically work with Australian and Asian investors, and I help them to own U.S. real estate in a passive, safe and profitable way.

What sets me apart: I began my personal real estate investing in 2006 and was able to gain financial freedom in my 20s and avail myself of the best opportunities from all around the world. I have found this to be U.S. Commercial Real Estate investing. In particular, we are able to understand our international investors intricately, as we once were in their position.

Testimonial: "Kevin and Daniella have a special talent for finding property deals that provide both short- and long-term value. They are high-quality people who I've come to know and trust, and the level of analysis and feedback they provide on my investment is exceptional. I have already invited several friends to join me in investing with them, and I would encourage you to do so too!" –N. Bailey, Australia

How to get in touch with me:
Email: daniella@dhillonpartners.com
Website: www.DhillonPartners.com

Social Media:
Facebook, LinkedIn

Scan here to learn more:

Lydia Monroy Helps Working Moms Have It All

Are you a mom that is a professional woman, CEO, or business owner who struggles with balancing career and motherhood? Would you like to create a passive income that can afford you the option to take time off with your family or children without going bankrupt? If you have found yourself awake in the middle of the night, wondering if you will have to sacrifice your family or your career, there is good news—you don't! Lydia Monroy wants you to know that it's possible to be a great mother and have a successful career without the guilt and without causing your home life to suffer. Lydia is a multifamily investment expert and co-founder of Pearl Equity Partners, LLC, a firm with investments from coast to coast. She has helped investors earn hundreds of thousands of dollars and now has her own firm and is empowering moms of all types to continue serving in the role that's most important to them while growing a financial empire. As a mother, Lydia knows how to balance it all and is eager to help you do the same.

Conversation with Lydia Monroy

What is your company? And how do you help someone with regard to real estate investing?

Lydia: My company is Pearl Equity Partners, LLC, and we acquire, transform and manage multifamily apartment communities. We focus on underperforming and underutilized value-add properties that are typically too small for institutional capital and too large for individual investors to buy. We help investors achieve a reliable and consistent return on their investment while limiting their liability and risk as a limited partner in the investment.

Could you describe the name or how would you classify your asset class? Your area of specialty?

Lydia: I would classify my specialty as multifamily value-add investing. The asset class, typically, is Class B, workforce housing properties.

Where do you invest, and what type of investments have you invested in?

Lydia: We invest across the U.S. My partner is my father-in-law, and he's based out of Washington, D.C., and I'm based out of Los Angeles. We have invested in properties in the D.C. metro area, which includes Maryland and Virginia. We've also invested in the Midwest in Michigan and Ohio and also out West from Southern California to Wyoming.

What type of investments have you invested in?

Lydia: We both have long histories of investing in real estate. I personally have invested in multifamily apartment communities anywhere from four to five units all the way up to hundreds of units, and my partner has extensive experience in multifamily as well as office properties.

Who is your ideal investor?

Lydia: Professional women and mothers who are looking to put their money to work for them. As women, we may have many demands, from our families to our careers to our philanthropic commitments. And we want more time to do the things we love and be present.

What type of success can you help your investors or clients achieve?

Lydia: Investing with us provides the opportunity to grow your wealth with a reliable, consistent passive income stream so that you can spend more time doing the things you love.

Can you share a little bit about what's unique about you as a professional or an investor that's different from others who offer similar services?

Lydia: Our approach to real estate investing is different from many firms. We don't rely on significant transactional events or unpredictable market timing to generate returns. Instead, our strategy emphasizes immediate, dependable and growing cash flow. This allows us to reduce risk and mitigate volatility for our investors. We have decades of experience in investing in over $2 billion in real estate throughout our careers.

So, tell us a little bit about your company, your focus, and how investing in real estate can enhance change and positively impact a woman's life.

Lydia: At Pearl Equity Partners, we are passionate about transforming communities. We look for underperforming assets that are not managed well and are in need of physical modernization. We bring rents to current market rates by executing on market proven value-add capital expenditure programs that typically involve unit upgrades with enhanced interior finishes and appliances and revitalized exteriors and common areas. The result is transformed apartments, a renewed community for residents, and better returns for our investment partners. By investing with us, you know your money is going to be put to work, improving the lives of others, providing a wonderful community for the residents to live, work, and play. Furthermore, it provides you, the investor, a reliable source of passive income that frees you up to do more of the things you love.

What types of investment opportunities do you offer to investors? And how much is required for an initial investment?

Lydia: We offer the opportunity to invest with us in multifamily assets as a limited partner where your liability and your risk is limited to your investment, and you receive an 8 to 12 percent return on your investment annually. Our minimum investment amount is $25,000.

What kind of return on investment do your projects offer, and typically how long does it take to recoup that investment?

Lydia: Our projects average an annual 8 to 12 percent cash returns during the hold period, and depending on the business strategy of the assets, it could take 5 to 10 years to receive all of your equity back. We are looking for assets we can improve and hold for the long term as we increase the cash flow and not quick market timed flips.

Why is investing in real estate advantageous to women and specifically multifamily investing?

Lydia: Investing in real estate provides an opportunity to have passive income where the returns are excellent, and it's less volatile compared to the stock market. And real estate is also a tangible asset you can visit at any time; you can see the impact of your investment and how it's improved the community and the neighborhood. It's also a reliable source of income, as workforce housing will always be in demand as demographic shifts continue. Even in a recession, people will still need a place to live. So, while the rents and returns may decrease temporarily, the asset won't be lost if it has been run responsibly by an experienced team.

Great. And what is the benefit again of working with you as a multifamily investment expert?

Lydia: You're teaming up with experienced investors that have built their firm on integrity and always doing the right thing. You can be confident in our abilities to execute on a business plan, provide transparency in financial and operating reporting that clearly demonstrates how the asset is performing. In addition, we have invested in a technology platform for investors so they can invest, review, and manage their investments as easily as they do with their bank accounts. We are not a large Wall Street firm where you might have limited access to the decision makers. We're available to investors and provide tours, info sessions, and educational opportunities so our investors can be more informed and confident.

What do you feel are the myths when it comes to investing in real estate?

Lydia: I think it's not knowing enough or not having enough time. Many people think that they need to buy their own rental properties, which takes significant equity and can be risky. So, of course, they want to be well informed and educated before making a purchase, which takes time. And then once they own the property, they need to make the time available to manage the asset and deal with all the issues that arise. Even if they hire a management company, it still takes significant time setting up protocols, approving requests, reviewing financials, etc. The time and knowledge required prevents many from investing directly into real estate. However, there is another option to be a direct owner as a passive limited equity partner with investment firms like Pearl Equity Partners.

What are some common misconceptions around the real estate industry, especially since the 2008 market crash, that are not true today? And why is now a good time to invest in real estate?

Lydia: Some misconceptions may be that investments are over-leveraged or risky. Underwriting for banks are more conservative today than they were in the past, and you rarely see the overleveraging where investors were able to put in little to nothing of their own equity into purchasing a property. Our underwriting standards are conservative, and we look for properties that are well built and are well located that will have demand throughout the years. We make conservative assumptions on growth and sales prices, and we test our model to ensure that in a recession or worst-case scenario, the property will still perform.

Gotcha! And what are some of the most common fears you've found that women have about getting started in real estate investing?

Lydia: I think it's that they don't know enough. As women, we want to figure it out, read, learn and have enough knowledge so that we invest responsibly. This is a wonderful way to operate; however, at the same time, it can lead to not taking action.

Yeah. And how can real estate investing make life better?

Lydia: Well, it can provide a supplemental income so that you can continue to grow your portfolio so you can eventually reduce the hours you work or, better yet, retire early. It's also a great opportunity to build wealth that you can pass down to future generations.

If they don't believe they have access to capital, what are some suggestions you would offer?

Lydia: One of the best suggestions I can offer is that they can pool their money with other family members or friends, and they can invest together through one entity such as an LLC. That way, they can have access to these types of investment opportunities that Pearl Equity Partners and other sponsors provide.

How can you help a woman who is interested in real estate investing achieve the greatest success?

Lydia: For a woman who's interested in investing in real estate, there are multiple options such as office, retail, hospitality, and multifamily. Each has its own risks that need to be addressed. However, in my opinion, multifamily as an asset class is less risky, especially with the changes in the economy and in a recession scenario. As I mentioned before, there is a consistent demand for multifamily housing. People will always need a place to live and especially in workforce housing. This area of Class B properties does well in a recession. In addition, there's consistent demand, from the millennials all the way to baby boomers who are retiring and looking to downsize. It's an asset class that's in more demand and less risky than other asset classes, which will help as you build your portfolio or your income stream and invest for the long term.

Can you share a story about one of your investors and a success that they accomplished investing with you?

Lydia: We have many women investors that are in various phases of their life, and I'll just mention a couple that invested with us recently. We have a professional single mother that's looking to supplement her income. We have an executive woman, with a goal of retiring early so she can travel once her kids graduate from high school. And we also have a retired grandmother that is looking to leave a legacy for her daughters and granddaughters. All of these women are achieving their earning goals by investing in real estate with us and earning a passive income.

What inspired you to become a real estate investor? And why multifamily investing?

Lydia: Prior to going to business school, I was in the nonprofit fundraising industry, and as I was out raising funds, I met with a number of successful people. Many were in real estate and encouraged me to get into the game and build wealth so that I could give back financially. I was also inspired by the many stories I heard of how people built significant wealth in one generation from multifamily investing. I decided to go for it. I went back to business school and made the career switch into real estate.

Tell us more about why you like real estate investing.

Lydia: I'm really interested in transforming lives and communities. I see investing in real estate as access to make a tangible difference, creating a community that people love to live in. In addition, I enjoy being able to deliver a return on our investors' funds to provide a consistent, reliable income stream that enables them to have more time and freedom to do the things they love.

Let's talk about a lesson that you learned early on as an investor that makes you a more valuable real estate investor today to work with.

Lydia: As I mentioned before, as women, we like to figure things out before making a move, to have the confidence that we will be successful, and I did exactly that in my career. While I worked at my prior firm, I learned the business inside and out. I helped to grow the firm from a few hundred million in assets to almost $1.8 billion assets in six years. With all that expertise, it wasn't until 2014 that I started investing in my own properties, and then it wasn't until 2017 that I made the leap to investing other people's money alongside my own. I learned that I could have done that much earlier and didn't have to wait until I gained a certain level of expertise or do it alone. Now that I have my own firm, I'm building the best team possible, from employees to consultants to property management to construction teams to lawyers and accountants. I operate my firm as a billion-dollar investment firm, and our investors benefit from not only my expertise but also the expertise of our collective team.

Is there anything further you'd like to add about obstacles or maybe overcoming some of the misconceptions that maybe you had before jumping in?

Lydia: Another obstacle would be that it takes a lot of money to invest in real estate. One of the first investments that I did on my own was buying a fourplex, where I utilized an FHA loan and put down three percent in equity. This was a rehab project, so I was also able to borrow money for the capital improvements. Within two years, I was able to completely transform the property and double the value. I then refinanced out of the FHA loan into a traditional loan and used the proceeds to not only pay off the construction loan that I had but also to pay off all my debt—student loans, car loan, and all my credit card debt. It was a home run, and I had additional proceeds available to invest in my next project.

What's the most important question women should ask themselves as they consider where they are today, where they want to be tomorrow, and how they plan to get there?

Lydia: I think one of the most important questions they should ask themselves is, where can I create teamwork in my life? We cannot achieve our goals alone; so, what can I take off my plate and enroll others to do so that I can have more time available to fulfill on the goals that are most important to me? Whom can I have on my team to achieve those goals? That's everyone, from friends and family to business relationships and people you just met. You never know who the person sitting next to you is and whom they know that can help you. So, it boils down to having clearly defined goals and then sharing them with others. When you're passionate and clear about what you want, you can then employ the services of others and inspire them to help you; then you can achieve your goals faster with freedom and ease.

What three qualities should a woman who's reading your chapter consider when they're choosing a real estate investor to work with?

Lydia: I think the three most important qualities that a woman should look at when they're looking to partner with another real estate sponsor are their integrity, their experience, and transparency.

For a woman who might say, "I'm already earning six figures" or "This sounds good, but I don't have the bandwidth to add anything else to my plate," why should she still consider adding real estate investing to her portfolio?

Lydia: Investing in real estate alongside individuals who have experience, you have the ability to put your money to work with limited time needed. In addition, you can build your wealth and take your financial success to the next level. So, what person making six figures doesn't want to make seven figures?!

How can someone find out more about you and your real estate opportunity?

Lydia: Yes, they can go to our website, pearlequitypartners.com, or connect with me on LinkedIn.

About Lydia Monroy

Company: Pearl Equity Partners, LLC

Who I can help: Women who want to grow their wealth with a reliable, consistent passive income stream so that they can spend more time doing the things they love.

What sets me apart: I'm a seasoned Real Estate Investor with over $2 billion in transactional experience. I'm an entrepreneur who values integrity, diversity, transparency, teamwork, and technology. I'm a mother who understands the demands of a career and family life and is committed to empowering others to have it all with power, freedom, and ease.

How to get in touch with me:
Email: lmonroy@pearlequitypartners.com
Website: PearlEquityPartners.com

Social Media:

LinkedIn.com/in/lydia-monroy-pearl-equity-partners

Scan here to learn more:

Two-for-One Investment Strategy: Don't Let the Credit System Stop You

Have you been trying to figure out how to buy your own home or desire to purchase an investment property, but your credit isn't great? Do you know that there is a way that you can do both? I know what you're probably thinking: *I don't have the money to afford my own home AND purchase an investment property.* Or maybe, *How can I afford a primary residence and an investment property?* LA-based investor Zabrina Horton is here to let you know you can have it all. As the founder of Dream Worthy Investments, Zabrina specializes in 'two-for-one' investing: owning your own home and renting out the other side, investments of 2–4 units, or purchasing a 2–4-unit duplex in a state with great cash flow.

In addition to teaching clients how to find multi-purpose and multi-unit investment properties, Zabrina simultaneously helps her clients increase their credit score, which increases your purchasing power. She helps prospective investors understand the credit system and how to make the changes necessary to increase their score so they qualify for more to get started investing in real estate. Worried that your credit isn't high enough to invest? Intrigued by the idea of making money off your home while you live in it? Read on to discover how Zabrina can guide you into becoming a homeowner and real estate investor and receive cash flow each month with this method.

Conversation with Zabrina Horton

Tell us about your company, your focus, and how investing in real estate can enhance, change and positively impact a woman's life.

Zabrina Horton: What my company does is help with credit repair. More specifically, though, we dispute the negative items that come up on your credit report. This can help women in a variety of ways, especially when it comes to required down payments on things like real estate investments, homes, or cars. Lower down payments lead to lower interest rates—which, in turn, can save you money.

I believe that there is a plethora of information out there, as well as secrets or tips, that people don't know about. I provide the information and recommendations to my clients and help them find the companies that can assist with things like student loans or loan debt.

What types of investments opportunities do you offer, and how much is required for an initial investment?

Zabrina Horton: I offer opportunities for clients to make money on their investments through single-family home flips. I also teach clients to expect making a return on their investment in two-to four-unit buy-and-holds.

The initial investment cost varies: investments can be as low as $5,000 for someone who is just starting out, to give them confidence. From there on, the increments can increase to $10,000, then $50,000, and then $100,000.

What kind of return on investment (ROI) do your projects offer, and typically how long does it take to recoup an investment?

Zabrina Horton: There really is no standard, but a typical ROI is around ten percent. So, for example, if someone invested $5,000, then they would make $500. Our investments start giving returns as soon as three months or can give returns one year out from the initial investment.

Why is investing in real estate advantageous for women—specifically with your two-for-one strategy or your two to four multi-family investments?

Zabrina Horton: First and foremost, investing in real estate provides independence. I think, down the road, though, that it can create a legacy—something that we can leave to our next generations. A lot of younger generations are not thinking about that, so I feel like it's our duty to educate them because this is not only our legacy but theirs as well.

What is the benefit of working with you as an investor?

Zabrina Horton: I think the biggest reason is my level of experience: I have worked in the entertainment industry as a publicist for over twenty-five years. For twelve of those years, I worked at BET Networks as a Sr. PR Manager, and then I had my first baby at age forty-eight. When I came back from maternity leave, though, my position was eliminated, and I was laid off. Since then, I have been investing in different real estate asset classes and have a good bit of experience with it. I look at it as a blessing because now I'm doing something that I've always wanted to do; plus, I'm not as stressed out!

Another benefit is that I look at my properties as a safety net and want my clients to have the same kind of security. My properties serve me as an ATM—they make money for me. This means if there's an emergency, and I need cash, I can take the money out of my house or out of my duplex. I have options. I will still get paid monthly by my tenants, which means that I always get a paycheck, no matter what. With that extra security and a safety net, if, God forbid, you get laid off or something happens that affects your primary source of income, you can move on with less worry or anxiety.

What do you feel are the biggest myths when it comes to investing in real estate?

Zabrina Horton: In my experience, there are a lot of myths. People think that they can't afford a house or that it's too much work. However, over the years, rent has risen so much that it has overtaken the cost of a mortgage. So, in the long-run, investing in real estate is much more prudent than dumping money into rent, and then that money is gone forever.

Another popular myth is that you can't get a house if your credit score is too low. We work with clients to fix this in multiple ways. First, we push educating yourself: our client needs to know what their score is, how to analyze it and to know how credit works. Knowing and education can go a long way. The second thing that we do is learn how to rebuild the credit. Clients should keep in mind that it takes about three months but that we do know the tips and tricks that raise the score in those three months immensely.

What are some common misconceptions around the real estate industry, especially since the 2008 market crash, that are not true today? And why is now a good time to invest in real estate?

Zabrina Horton: Many real estate circles say that the best time to invest was between ten and thirty years ago. The next best time to invest in real estate is today.

The crash affected both the stock and housing markets heavily. However, it ended up affecting the stock market much more. Those that were in the housing market were adequately prepared and, therefore, were able to work fine through the crash. Some people in the housing market were affected and went upside down in their homes, but generally, the housing market is safe from dips and turns in the market.

It is important to remember, though, that things are different now than they were before the crash. The government and banks both have instituted new policies and procedures and are now careful to ensure that we don't repeat the same mistakes. These are also great because if a crash happens again, it's less likely to be that devastating. Instead of driving off a cliff, it's hitting a little dip in the road.

What are some of the most common fears you have found that women have about getting started in real estate investing?

Zabrina Horton: One of the biggest fears is something that I have personally been through: thinking that you have no idea what you are doing. This can be extremely overwhelming, but you just take one step at a time and have to realize that you are not alone.

In real estate, it is important to work with experts that you trust. There are always plenty of educated people to talk to. Personally, I talk to my mortgage loan officer; he's an investor, flipper and knows about money. I talk to him or other investors and ensure that I keep learning. A lot of people think that real estate is something that you can do by yourself; it isn't, though. You need multiple people as far as investing is concerned: an agent, a mortgage broker, an attorney. If your credit isn't good, in addition, you will need a credit repair service.

I think another big fear is that of the unknown. You don't know what is going to happen, but that fear is normal and human: everyone has this fear. How you push through that, though, and get to the other side is through increasing your knowledge base. You should always be learning—you should always grow in your knowledge.

I attend different seminars as well and have done that since before the crash. That's when I learned a lot about the job and about different financing options: self-directed retirement funds, self-directed IRAs. These are two things that are not common knowledge. That's why constantly learning and networking is crucial. There are so many avenues and paths that you can go about to make money and increase your wealth in real estate.

How can real estate investing make life better?

Zabrina Horton: In my opinion, a sense of relief and a sense of security go together; you want to make sure that you are prepared, just in case you lose your job. If, God forbid, you lose your job, one option is maybe you can sell your house—you can sell it because you have an asset that has a lot of value, just from paying your mortgage every month, or better yet, having your tenants do it. It's money that's going right into your bank account for YOU in case of emergency.

How can you help a woman who is interested in buying her first home, interested in your two-for-one strategy, or is interested in purchasing a two-to-four-unit investment property achieve the greatest success?

Zabrina Horton: There's an idea that was once introduced to me that I would like to introduce to someone starting out: live where you want but invest where it makes sense.

For example, I live in California, which is very expensive when buying property, whether your own home or rental property. It doesn't matter. It's expensive. But when compared to Detroit, where I also invest, there is a huge difference. I always use the example of shopping: California is Neiman Marcus; Detroit is TJ Maxx or Ross. If I went into Neiman Marcus, I could maybe buy one dress on the clearance rack. At Ross or TJ Maxx however, I can go in, buy a whole entire outfit, OR TWO, including shoes, jewelry, a purse, scarf, perfume, a collection of hats if it's Easter. I can buy all of that and still have some money left over.

If you want to create a revenue stream, the barrier of entry is a LOT lower—mostly because it's less expensive to purchase or invest.

I mean, you can purchase a home outright! Growing up in California, buying a house outright was unheard of to me until I went to my first out-of-state investing seminar. One thought process is that you can continue to pay rent in LA for a little while and own a property out of state, collecting rent from it. Now, that property out of state is going toward your rent in LA or whatever your hometown is. In two years or so, you could take the money out of the house and buy a home here in LA—or buy that Neiman Marcus dress.

Right now, Detroit is making a comeback. It's still very affordable because there are still a lot of abandoned houses that need to be demolished. So, I am investing in Detroit, where it's going to make sense, and I can buy multiple properties and increase my money over and over.

Can you share a story about one of your investors and a success that they accomplished investing with you?

Zabrina Horton: As far as a success story, everything is still in the making. Right now, we are past the initial stages and have gotten our feet into the water. By the time this book is out, we've jumped in. We're not just testing the waters; we are in them.

What inspired you to become a real estate investor, and why the dual-purpose properties or two to four-unit investments?

Zabrina Horton: The person that inspired me the most was my grandmother; we called her Mama Rocksy. She, my grandfather, and my father raised me. She was a music teacher and a landlady throughout my childhood. Mama Rocksy was active in the community in Pasadena, California, and was on the board of directors of housing organizations for people of color, which little did I know then would have such a profound effect on me. She owned six or seven houses, and my cousins and I are just now selling the last one. We say that the legacy of Mama Rocksy lives on, though, since we see the proceeds from the sale as a gift from her to her grandchildren. When I was a small child, she planted this seed in me, which continues to inspire me to help other people realize the value of real estate.

Another part of my purpose deals with my three-year-old son, Michael Jackson. He is my inspiration every day. When I see him, I see how the world is moving forward with technology, and the jobs are changing. Everything is so much more technical, which leads to a need to diversify. This leads to wanting more and striving for more—reaching for the sky. I think that it's a much stronger reason to look at doing more in your life than barely surviving, making just enough to pay the bills, and always wishing you can do things and go places.

I think my inspiration is helping young people make good decisions with their money and future. Right now, a lot of these young folks want to make it in the entertainment industry and ask me to mentor them. So, I work with them from a dual standpoint of entertainment and investment, stressing the importance that they have their legacy set up and they are financially secure.

Can you share a lesson you learned early on as an investor that makes you a more valuable real estate investor today to work with?

Zabrina Horton: As far as credit is concerned, I learned a lesson in having a high debt to income ratio, also known as a DTI.

At the beginning of my real estate journey, I had to pay off a couple of creditors to lower my DTI. This is a very important part of your credit report. Something that I learned was that once those things are off your credit report, you now have the money that you would have been putting toward these bills as income that can be put toward real estate purchases.

This is knowledge that someone older might think is basic, but for recent college graduates and younger people, they may not know how to balance their DTI. They have a car payment that might be four to five hundred dollars a month, and that's a big chunk or even an entire paycheck, you know? So, it's important to learn about debt to income ratio and how to balance the two well.

That's not to say that you should feel bad; you should be able to relax and do things that 'twenty-somethings' do. You just need to know how not to waste your money. Have fun and live your life but have your money in order. To play, you must work. After you get your business in order, then you can have even more fun, and then you can be the real VIP.

What's the most important question women should ask themselves as they consider where they are today, where they want to be tomorrow, and how they plan to get there?

Zabrina Horton: First, I think that you must ask that exact question: Where do I want to be in five years?

You must think ahead … beyond just this or next year. Think five years ahead. This is YOUR life; so, instead of worrying about the latest celebrities—what Cardi B or the Kardashians are doing—you should worry about your own life. This is YOUR reality show episode, your song, your movie.

What are three qualities that a woman reading your chapter should consider when choosing a real estate investor to work with?

Zabrina Horton: I would say that the first quality would be clarity: you need someone that can speak clearly, in a way that you can understand. There are a lot of acronyms and terminology in real estate investment, so you need to have someone on your team that can explain them in clear language.

The other two qualities go together: professionalism and experience. The longer you have been in the game, the more professionally you will conduct yourself. You need someone that is going to be there for you every step of the way and is going to care about your success and take care of you.

So, for a woman who might say, "I'm already earning six figures," or for a woman who might say, "This sounds good, but I don't have the bandwidth to add anything else to my plate," why should she still consider adding real estate investing to her portfolio?

Zabrina Horton: Generally, there are two main types of investors: active and passive. And while they are wildly different, they can be adjusted to fit anyone's timeframe or mindset.

Passive investors are just as the name suggests: they don't really do any of the work. It requires almost no time, except the time to listen to the opportunity and ask questions. You don't have to say 'yes' right away, and it only takes a few hours—you don't even have to put any brain power into it. In a few years, though, the money will compound—or grow—without you doing a single thing! It grows on its own without you having to work on it.

Active investors, as well, is just as it sounds. The active investor puts in something called 'sweat equity'—this simply means their wealth comes from their work. They are the ones that are out there sweating, putting together a deal, negotiating—doing everything from A to Z. They are the ones who do work and spend time at it as if it was their job.

How can someone find out more about you and your real estate opportunities?

Zabrina Horton: To take advantage of credit repair services, my website is MyFes.net/zhorton. To learn more about our investment opportunities in Detroit, go to DetroitDreamIS.com.

About Zabrina Horton

Company:
Dream Worthy Investments

Who I can help: We work with both men and women entrepreneurs, as well as those that want to repair their credit, to create opportunities and financially prepare for tomorrow.

What sets me apart: I am a TV publicist turned real estate investor. Meaning, not only do I make money, I help others make money too. I use my PR skills to bring people and deals together, making strategic, profitable partnerships.

How to get in touch with me:
Email: zabrina@DetroitDreamIS.com
Website: MyFes.net/zhorton and DetroitDreamIS.com

Social Media:

Facebook.com/zabrinahorton

Twitter.com/zabrinahorton

Instagram.com/zabrinahorton

Scan here to learn more:

Women Are Living Longer: Investment Opportunities That Can Outlast Retirement Income That Are Also Purpose-Driven

Did you know that people are living longer, women are living longer than men, and people are living longer than their retirement savings and income? Have you ever considered the possibility of your life outliving your income? Would you like to invest in real estate projects and receive great returns while making a difference in the world? Dr. Felecia Froe can help ensure that you have solid wealth and wellness plans in place. Dr. Froe is part of a team that manages over $100 million in investments. Her purpose-driven approach to real estate investing, along with her expertise and commitment to helping women build wealth and offering them advice on wellness through her company 18 Seconds for Health, makes her a unique real estate investment coach.

Whether you want to replace your current income, are approaching retirement, desire to be a part of something bigger than yourself while making passive income or simply wish to build an income that will supplement your retirement, Dr. Froe has investments designed specifically for women. These investment opportunities will help you build wealth, and with the 18 Seconds for Health initiative, you will also receive the benefit of learning how to communicate better with your doctors to help maintain your and your family's well-being physically, mentally, and emotionally. Explore working with Dr. Froe for real estate investment opportunities that are tied to helping others while building a legacy for your family.

Conversation with Dr. Felecia Froe

Dr. Froe, tell us about your company, your focus, and how investing in real estate can enhance, change, and positively impact a woman's life.

Dr. Felecia Froe: Narwhal Investment Group is a private investment firm which provides professional women the opportunity to take control of their lives financially. We believe if you're working to live a longer life but are not getting financially prepared for that, you're only getting the job half done.

We focus on helping you understand why we feel real estate should be a substantial part of your portfolio. We find, evaluate and offer purpose-driven investments to give you a superior return, especially when compared to many Wall Street options.

While we want every investment to give investors a monetary return, we also want to improve the community where the real estate is located. We choose value-added projects, with the goal of improving the property or business, as well as community, as well as provide a return on the investment and ultimately return of capital. By donating a part of our profit to a charitable investment partner who matches our philosophy, we work to improve the world by improving the lives of women and children and serve a bigger purpose.

What types of investment opportunities do you offer, and how much is required for an initial investment?

Dr. Felecia Froe: Currently, we work with multiple types of real estate: residential assisted living communities, international agriculture, and multifamily buildings. We are now working on hotel projects and are researching new opportunities with hydroponics.

At this time, the amount needed to participate in an investment can range from $25,000 to $100,000. On these investments, you can expect to begin receiving returns between three months and a year from your initial investment.

Therefore, it is important for us to know what your financial needs and wants are before we work together. Our group wants you to succeed with your investments and transform your life—along with the lives of others. We want to align your needs with your investments; this gives you both a great return and helps to meet your higher needs and goals.

What kind of Return on Investment (ROI) do your projects offer, and typically how long does it take to recoup an investment?

Dr. Froe: Over the life of the investment, the projects that we offer will generate between eight and twenty percent returns per year. As a note, for some investments, 'returning your capital' does not automatically put you out of the deal; you may continue to receive the passive income for as long as we hold the property or business.

Why is investing in real estate advantageous to women, and can you share more about your Profitable Investments with A Purpose?

Dr. Felecia Froe: There are many reasons why real estate investing is advantageous to your portfolio.

Number one: taxes. Taxes are the biggest expenses of our lifetime. If done properly, however, real estate investing can minimize or eliminate much of your tax liability. U.S. tax law is written to be advantageous to both real estate and business investors. To know exactly how to take advantage of this benefit, though, you must have a good accountant on your team and use them to understand the tax advantages and disadvantages of all of your investments and spending decisions.

Number two: cash flow. Real estate can give you both passive income and the potential for infinite returns. Real estate investments can be leveraged—meaning you can use someone else's money to buy it. This improves your return because if the property is bought wisely, there is money left over after all expenses are paid, including the mortgage. This is your cash flow.

Investing With a Purpose is about giving: it gives us a higher reason to do what we do. We all desire meeting certain needs: security, a home, love and belonging, feeling a sense of accomplishment. Our investment opportunities can fulfill all these needs. You can get a sense of security and have money working for you, so you can achieve your passive income goals.

In addition, we aspire, with your help, to improve the world. A portion of the profits from each of our investments goes to work for one of our charitable investment partners. Generally, we pick these investment partners from a pool of organizations that help make women and children more self-reliant.

What do you feel are the biggest myths when it comes to investing in real estate?

Dr. Felecia Froe: Myth number one is thinking, *I don't know enough.*

A study by Merrill Lynch shows that women felt equal, if not more confident than men, when it comes to budgeting and paying bills. But we feel significantly less confident when it comes to investing. This is perhaps due to women feeling more risk-averse. Our company is designed to help you become more educated about the risks associated with different types of investments, thereby helping you feel more confident in your ability to invest.

Number two is thinking, *I must spend a lot of time.*

Initially, you have to spend more time educating yourself. But I think of it like having your first child: you feel so incompetent and worry that you will screw up. We read, we ask experts, and we educate ourselves. Along the way, we may mess up, but we learn from that. It's the same thing with investing. The first investment is scary; you read, ask friends, ask them more, then read more. It takes both time and headspace. Finally, though, you invest, and it either goes well or not. Either way, you learn and then do it again, which is not as scary. Now you're on a roll.

Number three is thinking, *I don't have enough money.*

Whatever funding you have, we will help you find it and use it to expand your financial ability. We are not about denying yourself through investing; we are about growing your money in order to live the life that you deserve.

What are some common misconceptions around the real estate industry, especially since the 2008 market crash, that are not true today? And why is now a great time to invest in real estate?

Dr. Felecia Froe: I think one of the biggest misconceptions is thinking that everyone lost money; this isn't true. Those that were in proper positioning didn't lose anything; in fact, many of them prospered. I admit that I lost a lot of money at the time, but I learned a great lesson.

Through that, I've become a better investor, which helps me manage the money better. One of the biggest takeaways is that investing is a team sport. With my team and network, I feel prepared to not only survive the next downturn but thrive through it.

I think now is a good time to invest in real estate due to where we are in the market cycle. Assets that are properly positioned will do well through a downturn and will also give cash flow through the long-term.

What are some of the most common fears you have found that women have about getting started in real estate investing?

Dr. Felecia Froe: The most common fear is the thought of losing money. We all want a guaranteed winner. In general, women know how to save; when it comes to investing, though, we tend to let someone else handle it. We often put our money into the stock market and let someone else handle it. We should remember that no one cares about our money and future more than we do.

Keep in mind that statistics show that most of us will be financially responsible for ourselves and perhaps our children. Forty-seven percent of women over fifty are single. In addition, it is estimated that only twenty percent of Baby Boomer women will be financially secure in their retirement. You don't need to be one of these women. It's time for us to change this statistic.

How can real estate investing make life better?

Dr. Felecia Froe: Investing in real estate can make life better by providing passive income. Passive income is money coming in, whether or not you go to work. More passive income than your expenses equals financial freedom. Financial freedom means you are truly free and you are able to wake up every day and choose what to do.

In addition to what this can do for you, think about what it can do for others. Imagine your children seeing you financially free. Imagine how that will affect them and their lives.

I believe that Narwhal Investment Group can help by working to educate women about various investment options and providing a place to invest. Women are investing in real estate and doing well. When we see that another woman with the same fears is succeeding, we gain confidence.

When you invest with me, you will be helping other women and children through the donation of part of our profits to organizations that help raise their quality of life. The ripple effect of you learning to invest is enormous.

What are the benefits of working with you as an investor?

Dr. Felecia Froe: There are multiple benefits to working with me and the Narwhal Investment Group. One of the biggest is that we spend time with you. We work to understand your investment goals and the legacy that you wish to leave. Once we've determined that, we can help you place capital into projects that work to meet all of your goals.

Our goal at Narwhal Investment Group is to improve your well-being.

How can you help a woman who is interested in finding investment opportunities achieve the greatest success?

Dr. Felecia Froe: One of the biggest blind spots is often finding the capital; we simply can't see beyond the usual ways to get money. I think that short-sighted attitude puts the wrong wording in our head. We say "I can't afford it" instead of "How can I afford it?" This small change changes our perception and gets us to start thinking of a solution.

Can you share a story about one of your investors and a success that they accomplished working with you?

Dr. Felecia Froe: I've been working with a woman who just had a baby girl and was told she should work until the baby was eighteen. She loves her job but wanted the option of taking time off now. After several conversations about her goals, we were able to decrease her tax burden through real estate investing.

This is important because taxes are our biggest expense. When we decreased her tax payments, we were able to free up more money to invest in cash-flowing real estate projects, with decreased taxable income. Now, she is on her way to building a passive income portfolio and, shortly, will be able to choose what days she is at work.

What inspired you to become a real estate investor, and why are your investments attached to both profit and purpose?

WEALTH FOR WOMEN · 145

Dr. Felecia Froe: Initially, I got interested through the book *Rich Dad Poor Dad* given to me by a woman business owner in the early 2000s while working on a real estate project. I read the book but didn't take the plunge quite yet. However, another woman who happened to be my patient was in my office one day; she was young and seemed like she could come to the office any time. When I asked what she did, she told me she was a real estate investor.

Shortly thereafter, I had the opportunity to invest in a property, and this woman came with me. She walked through the property with me, and she gave me the backup that I needed to get over the edge. That was all I needed. Since then, I have invested in many states, as well as internationally, as both an active and passive investor.

I believe that we are here for something bigger than ourselves. I'm passionate about women's and children's issues and work with organizations that help people become self-reliant. We choose charitable investment partners with these characteristics: basically, those that are working to put themselves out of business.

Can you share a lesson you learned early on as an investor which makes you a more valuable real estate investor to work with today?

Dr. Felecia Froe: This same woman that helped me get my first investment helped with several others after. At some point, I stopped seeking her advice and eventually realized we were under-capitalized. We lost a lot of money, self-esteem, confidence—everything was lost. I believe what we did wrong was not having a team to talk to or actually help us see the downsides of anything. At the time, we could only see the upside. I learned my lesson. Now we have a team, people that help us figure out what can go wrong, and we work to mitigate.

What's the most important question women should ask themselves as they consider where they are today, where they want to be tomorrow, and how they plan to get there?

Dr. Felecia Froe: The biggest question that women need to ask is 'why.' "Why am I doing this?" "Why is this important to me?" Keep in mind, if the answer doesn't make you get up every day, then it isn't strong enough. Your reason is everything: if you have a strong reason, then things get easier; if you don't, then things can become very difficult.

Once you have your 'why' and a good sense of where you want to go, build and work with your team. Narwhal Investment Group will work with you and help you figure out how you can get from your financial point A to point Z as quickly as possible.

What three qualities should a woman reading your chapter consider when choosing a real estate investor to work with?

Dr. Felecia Froe: I would say that they should look for the same qualities that they look for in a doctor. You want to work with someone that you can trust, someone you can understand, and someone who takes the time and be transparent with you. I recommend putting your money with someone you can trust. You wouldn't give a bag of money to someone that you don't know and ask them to take it to the bank for you—you just wouldn't. It's honestly the same thing: you need to trust the person who will be in charge of your money.

So, for a woman who might say, "But I'm already earning six figures" or "That sounds great, but I don't have the bandwidth to add anything else to my plate," why should she still consider adding real estate investing to her portfolio?

Dr. Felecia Froe: I feel like both of these women—the six-figure salary earner and the stay-at-home mom—feel like they don't have enough bandwidth. I think that we are all very busy, but the thing that I want everyone to remember is that the number of women in poverty, especially as we age, is very high. Only twenty percent of female

Baby Boomer women will be financially secure in their retirement; fifty-eight percent of females have less than ten percent of what they need in retirement. Seven out of ten women will live some years of their life in poverty—and this isn't because we don't know about money.

This is mostly because we don't think about our own future: we think about everybody else, everything else. We fail to take care of ourselves, but we need to so that we can better take care of them and show them how to be self-sufficient.

To get around this, I encourage women to invest for themselves but think of doing it for someone else. Do it to show your children, to teach them how to be self-reliant, to become financially free, so that they can choose what they want to do every day of their lives.

About Dr. Felecia Froe

Name: Felecia Froe, MD

Company: Narwhal Investment Group, LLC

Who I can help: Women whose goal is to increase their passive income. You are concerned with your economic return on investments as well as the social return on your investment. You ask questions such as, "Besides me, who will this investment help?" Our goal is to help women around the world improve their status and, by doing so, improve the status of their communities. We want self-reliant, confident women.

What sets me apart: As a divorced black woman who became a urologist when there were less than 100 female urologists in the country; mother of multi-ethnic, millennial, entrepreneurial women; I am able to see a problem from multiple perspectives. My medical training has helped me to be able to help you 'diagnose' your situation. My investment career and education help me to provide a 'treatment' plan that suits you. Raising millennial, entrepreneurial children has taught me patience. My goals and aspirations are not your goals and aspirations. My practice is about helping you to achieve what you uniquely are working to achieve.

How to get in touch with me:
Email: Felecia@narhwalinvestmentgroup.com
Website: NarwhalInvestmentGroup.com

Social Media:
Twitter: @feleciafroemd
Instagram: 18secondsforhealth.com

Scan here to learn more:

For as Little as $2,500, You Can Start Owning Real Estate in One of the Fastest Growing Cities

Could you use a rebirth in your finances? Or maybe you would like to reinvent yourself and create passive streams of income. Well, this investment opportunity may be just for you. There are several signs that Detroit might be a golden goose: unemployment is down, the poverty rate is a full point below the national average, and population growth and development are booming. These are all signs of a great city to invest in.

Professionals are moving back to Detroit from more expensive cities. The median house value in Detroit has increased 40% since 2017. And if all of that isn't enticing enough, the owner of several sports franchises has been heavily investing in Detroit—and Deba Harper is just the woman you want to get on board with. Deba offers unique, turnkey opportunities with low-entry amounts needed to get started investing. With a degree in urban planning, and as the only black woman on the Salesforce team for the Detroit Land Bank Authority, the repository for all Detroit residential properties in the city, Deba has the inside scoop on what areas are hot in Detroit. There is no time like the present to learn about the real estate revitalization and real estate opportunities available in the Motor City.

Conversation with Deba Harper

Deba, tell us about your company, your focus and how investing in real estate can enhance, change and positively impact a woman's life.

Deba Harper: The company is Detroit D.R.E.A.M. Investment Solutions, and we offer opportunities for people to invest in Detroit real estate. D.R.E.A.M. is an acronym for Develop Real Estate and Asset Management, and we manage all operations of the development, from acquisition to lease-up and maintaining the asset's productive use. Passive investors seed their money with us—we nurture and grow it so they can reap the highest annualized dividends.

Our economic development projects improve the property value and the people value of the communities that we're in. It's important because so many people here in Detroit have lived here through the high and hard times. It's important that we create a community of inclusion where we can help the people who are living here grow. As we develop the property value, we can grow the people value and help them maintain the communities they have lived in for generations. We're taking undervalued assets and renovating them while also developing and driving the market by setting rental and home sell value at a stabilized market rate. We also are offering affordable housing solutions to help current populations in the community sustain housing security.

What types of investment opportunities do you offer, and how much is required for an initial investment?

Deba Harper: We make our investment affordable at many different levels for people to get into the real estate investment game. We have three levels of investment opportunities: our entry level is $2,500, and we accept investments beyond $50,000. Our 3 investment levels are Key Members, Block Club Members, and Visionary Partners.

What kind of return on investment (ROI) do your projects offer, and typically how long does it take to recoup an investment?

Deba Harper: Our investors share in the average growth. Gross annual returns averaging 30 percent, and their share is dependent on how much they originally invested. So, within two years, our investors begin to recoup their investment.

Why is investing in real estate advantageous to women in the entertainment industry and specifically turnkey investments in Detroit?

Deba Harper: I used to be an entertainment industry professional. We're always working overtime to meet deadlines, so when you are in a high energy profession like that, it's difficult to start developing real estate, especially outside of California. You know where the entertainment Mecca is, and for most, it is too expensive to invest in real estate there. So, if you start looking at investments that your dollar can impact, you're looking outside California. The learning curve to understand a market in another city could be steep, and it could also be overwhelming to understand how to make the most from your money.

Well, we solve that. You don't have to worry about impacting your schedule because by investing your money with Detroit DREAM Investment Solutions, we're doing all the work for you. If you think you don't have enough money, we've made it easy for you by having a Key Member level, which is a low-barrier to entering into real estate investing. By being a member of our group, you'll be able to learn what goes into a real estate development. As the project develops, your investor knowledge and confidence grows. Investing your disposable income into real estate makes your earnings work for you by generating positive revenue without compromising your career.

And what is the benefit of investing with you and in your turnkey opportunities?

Deba Harper: The benefit of investing in our turnkey investment is that we're in Detroit, and people have heard about how inexpensive it is to buy houses in Detroit. They've heard they can buy a house for as little as $500 or $1,000. But there are so many things that go into buying a house for $500. You must look at the condition of that house, how much it's going to take to make that house habitable, what the city regulates, and securing the property during renovation.

We know what goes into bringing a blighted house into productive use. Then we lease the property to the right tenant that will take care of that house. We do everything for the investor. Investing in our turnkey, you can trust that we do what we say we are going to do. We keep you informed, and every month, you'll get your money for your net cash flow from your investment.

What do you feel are the biggest myths when it comes to investing in real estate?

Deba Harper: The biggest myth is, "I don't have any clue." There're always opportunities to invest, even if you just want to do it at an entry point. The other is that "there is not an affordable investment where I can become a homeowner." Well, there might not be an affordable investment where you live, especially if you live in one of the more expensive metro cities like LA or New York. You might not see a place there where you can invest your money, but there are other communities and cities, like Detroit, that are a great place to grow your money.

What are some common misconceptions about the real estate industry, especially since the 2008 market crash, that are not true today? And why is now a good time to invest in real estate?

Deba Harper: Since the market has turned around, it's hard to find an affordable and fast investment to get in. So, people are looking around, thinking, *I can't afford to invest where I live.* Well, there are investments in Detroit or Cleveland or Atlanta that are more favorable. There are assets that you can invest in more cheaply than you could in California. This is the beauty of investing today: as of December 2017, the tax bill that was passed opened up something called opportunity zones where you can invest your money, and for 10 years, no taxes have to be paid on your capital gains.

What are some of the most common fears you have found that women have about getting started in real estate investing?

Deba Harper: I think the biggest fear that women have is second-guessing. I feel like women have a confidence level that they feel like real estate investment is a man's job. They go to some of those seminars about how you could flip your house, and it's filled with men. You know, women are nurturers, so we like to keep it safe.

Real estate sometimes doesn't feel safe, even though it is safer than putting your money in a bank. The fact that you have a tangible asset means that a bank is going to give you a small return. And then you have to pay taxes on what you have in the bank, whereas with a real estate investment, you're getting a greater return, and you're getting a tax deduction. So, for women, we have to understand that sometimes your highest yield is long-term wealth by making investments that might seem risky. But women need to have confidence in themselves and their decision to put their money to work for them.

How can real estate investing make life better?

Deba Harper: Real estate investing makes a person's life better because they could be making money that they wouldn't ordinarily count on. We're going to work every day thinking that our job is secure, but the economic downturn showed us that nothing is secure. If we put our money into real estate—where everybody needs to have a place to live—you're making your money work for you.

Now you're investing in a community that is thriving. You now are making another level of money while you work, while you're in a traffic jam, while you're doing yoga, while you're birthing your child.

You can tap into that wealth that you're creating and not the money that you get from your salary and wages. Your real estate investment is now a tax deduction against your earnings, so your IRS refund is a bigger check.

So, Deba, it sounds like real estate investing is something more women should consider as a revenue stream and a way to stop trading time for money. I'm sure you've piqued some interest in what you've shared, but someone may be concerned as to where to find the money to invest in your projects if they don't believe they have access to capital.

How can you help a woman in the entertainment industry who is interested in turnkey investments achieve the greatest success?

Deba Harper: A turnkey investment is the best way to go for someone that might be limited on liquidity or extra capital. I know a lot of us who live paycheck-to-paycheck, but if we can sacrifice for a brand-new Gucci bag, then we can put some of that money aside or bring our friends together. If four or five friends put in $500, together you can invest in Detroit projects. Now you have a cash flow that's coming in every month instead of your money not working for you.

Women can come together. Women are communal people. We can sit around to talk and gossip about what's happening on a TV show— then we can come together and invest in something bigger like collective wealth building that changes our communities.

Can you share a story about one of your development projects and the success that was achieved?

Deba Harper: Well, honestly, my big success story is probably my partner, but I want to compare and contrast because both me and my partner, Zabrina Horton, came from the entertainment industry, and our lives are kind of parallel. We realized that we have the same friends, and we have a lot of professional similarities. After I came back from maternity leave, I was laid off. I wasn't investing in real estate. I was managing bands, investing in albums, but I wasn't putting any money away for myself. However, my partner put her money into a duplex in Los Angeles. When she was laid off three days after she returned from maternity leave, she had money that sustained her so she didn't have to take the package that they offered to her. Whereas, I was forced to take the offer, and within 6 months, I had to move out of my house and downsize my lifestyle. Within a year, I was living with my mother with a young child because I didn't prepare properly.

My journey afforded me the insight to see where the problems are in our society when we don't have housing security. I'm grateful for my journey of failed hopes that revived purposeful dreams to transform communities through urban planning and real estate development.

There is no doubt that investing in real estate is a way to create a nest egg of wealth that will cushion any life changes that might happen to you: losing your job, child college bills, medical issues, or even expanding your creativity. With passive revenue put away, you weather these life changes with the capital to maintain financial independence.

What inspired you to become a real estate developer, and why turnkey investments in Detroit specifically?

Deba Harper: Before being laid off from Mattel Toys, I was giving back to my community by hosting arts and education workshops in my backyard, called CAWT for Kids. During the economic downturn, I started noticing that the children were thinning out because their parents were losing their jobs and had to move because they had to sell their homes.

I started researching what the federal government was doing to recapture a failing middle class that was falling into poverty and homelessness. I became an advocate for housing at-risk and homeless youth under my non-profit, CHAMP Community Foundation. That's when I decided to go back to school and get my degree in urban planning. I wanted to realize my idea of a multi-income housing solution for community development. This concept was not favorable in Los Angeles because of the high market value. So I packed my Prius with my daughter and my dog. We drove to Detroit.

I was able to fit into the right position working for the Detroit Land Bank Authority, which is the repository of all residential parcels in Detroit. I was able to identify key markets where developments are happening. I feel like I've come to the right place to do some amazing things and grow a model that can be duplicated in other parts of Detroit and across the nation.

Can you share a lesson you learned early on as a developer that makes you a more valuable real estate developer today to work with?

Deba Harper: I was making near six figures in the entertainment industry, and I thought I was doing well. When I started investing, I realized my value perspective was small and that I needed to open my eyes to something much bigger than trading time for money—that there was an opportunity out there for me to have a bank account that had 50 million dollars, a hundred million dollars in it. I can make six figures, seven figures a year and invest in real estate. And I didn't have to be tied to a project or a computer. I can create a community that is functional; I can do shows all over the world if I wanted to because now I have the money to do it. It's just a bigger picture when you take your mind out of budgeting to what you're making at a job and expanding your thinking into what you can make by investing what you make at a job and leveraging in money-making ventures like real estate.

What's the most important question women should ask themselves as they consider where they are today, where they want to be tomorrow, and how they plan to get there?

Deba Harper: The biggest thing they should ask themselves is: what is their financial goal, and what is their value? Is there value in what they get paid for doing? Or is there value-added creativity that's within them that they want to bring forth in this world? Where is that money going to come from? Are you going to do that from what you get from your job and hope you get a promotion every year, or are you going to take a portion of your money and be able to invest in something that's gonna make you money while you're working at your job? What do you want to develop for the long term? What do you see as legacy wealth for yourself?

What three qualities should a woman reading your chapter consider in choosing a real estate developer to work with?

Deba Harper: "Do I like that person?" "Can I trust that person?" These are the top two questions because you're going to work with that person all the time. "Does this person I'm investing with know the market and the market potential?" "Does this person have a positive track record and business acumen and the capacity to deliver on what they promise?"

Again, I'm sure you've piqued some interest in your investment opportunities. So, for a woman who might say, "I'm already earning six figures" or "This sounds good, but I don't have the bandwidth to add anything else to my plate," why should she still consider adding real estate investing to her portfolio?

Deba Harper: You're not trading your time from being on your job. It's not impacting your bandwidth of time because Detroit DREAM Investment Solutions is doing all the work needed to grow your money so that you can have the greatest returns at the end of the year and have the biggest tax bracket to insure earning—it's a no-brainer.

How can someone find out more about you and your real estate opportunities?

Deba Harper: You can find out more about Detroit DREAM Investment Solutions by visiting our website DetroitDreamIS.com.

About Deba Harper

Company: Detroit DREAM Investment Solutions

Who I can help: Individuals with busy lives who are consumed by their careers and want to diversify their financial portfolio, millennials, social media moguls, and professional mothers working 16-hour days who use all their spare time to prioritize their families.

What sets me apart: I am a visionary, pioneer, and trailblazer who has been on the leading side of emerging technologies and industries my entire professional career. I recognized Detroit emerging from economic collapse to become 'American Comeback City.' Detroit has embraced me and my community development model. Together, we rise like the Phoenix.

Testimonial: "I wanted to let you know that I am so proud of you and impressed with the wealth of knowledge and wisdom you've gained about the Detroit Real Estate market in just a few short years. Your [Detroit DREAM - Investor Opportunity Session] presentation was stellar. I sat in amazement listening to you. Thank you for saving me a seat. I wish you great success and have no doubts you will reach the stars!" –Sheryl Mallory-Johnson, San Diego, CA

How to get in touch with me:
Email: deba@detroitdreamis.com
Website: DetroitDreamIS.com
CHAMP Community Foundation

Social Media:
Facebook.com/CHAMPNationOrg
LinkedIn.com/in/debaharper

Scan here to learn more:

The Person You Need to Keep and Close Your Real Estate Deals

Real estate investing is a team sport, and the members on your team can determine the outcome and success of your investing. Most people don't realize how important it is to have a real estate investing relationship expert to act as a liaison between you, your team, and the buyers and sellers you will be working with on your real estate investment transactions. Justine González has years of experience leading in school districts with consulting and communication and has perfected those communication skills to help real estate investors keep and close real estate deals. When hundreds of thousands of dollars are on the line, you want an experienced third-party liaison to close the communication gap and create positive outcomes that are beneficial to everyone involved. Justine has learned that good communication between buyers, sellers, and investment partners lead to greater overall success of a real estate transaction. As a real estate investor and facilitator, Justine offers investment opportunities that are win-win.

Conversation with Justine González

Tell us about you, your company, what you do and how you help real estate investors?

Justine González: Our company, Grayson and Gonzalez, offers various real estate investment opportunities for people who are interested in generating a passive income. Our main goal is to make the process for investing easy, whether it's your first deal or your 100th. So, when I think about being a coach to people, I think that it's necessary to have someone walk side-by-side with you in building success in real estate because it's all about the relationship. I personally have found that many new investors struggle to get outside of their comfort zone, and I help them with that.

I call myself a 'relationship coach,' which means that I primarily work with women that are new to real estate investing. Working together, we establish a plan to develop as well as leverage and sustain the relationships needed to reach their real estate investing goals.

I have developed a framework to support our newcomer clients; it's called VIP and ensures that my clients have their needs met personally while also providing them an ongoing plan of action for building, leveraging and sustaining relationships.

It is important for clients to understand that we are adding value back into their lives. This can also show them why it is so important that they go back to that, understand the commitment and see the value that it's building into their lives.

The bottom line is that real estate investing is all about numbers and, as a result, can become quite transactional instead of personal. To combat this, I provide coaching that helps women new to real estate investing gain success—by focusing on relational versus transactional. I think that beginning with relationships, listening is the key to being successful and having longevity with real estate investing. To help with this, I created a very personal solution to support newcomers from the time that they begin their journey.

What aspects of the investment process are you able to help clients with, keeping the idea of growing and building better relationships in mind?

Justine González: I work with women that are looking to be part of syndication, particularly in terms of asset classes. I also work with those that are interested in joint ventures and realize that you must be able to build trusting relationships with many team members. When it comes to syndication and larger deals, the reason why building these relationships is so important is that it gives you the option of being a passive investor. This means that you can leverage other people's money and time and have multiple people working with you to make the greater outcome. With syndication, though, there are a lot of moving parts. I want people to feel equipped to actually know how to manage these moving parts, as well as what they need to be aware of, because, at the end of the day, it's your money, so you want to make sure that these women are going into this one hundred percent confident. When you are giving your money to somebody, you always want the peace of mind that comes with feeling one hundred percent confident in who you are really working with and who you are giving your money to.

What makes you different to work with from other real estate investors?

Justine González: As I mentioned before, real estate investing is very transactional. When I came into this field, I was an educator and didn't really have that real estate background. At the time, I felt intimidated, surrounded by people that were coming from either business or financial sectors and not even understanding a lot of the language.

To work around this, I would read to just understand the most basic information of what an asset class is and what it indicates to you. In turn, I try to help solve these problems for people that are from other sectors to have the knowledge to get into the real estate sector. Clients can expect me to provide a highly personalized support and coaching system and then help them develop a firm foundation and relationships while creating a plan of action to reach their goals. I believe that with these supports in place, you are going to realize that you are not alone—because we are only as strong as the people whom we surround ourselves with.

One of the biggest myths is that you can do this on your own. If I'm honest, I really attempted to start my journey long ago, but I didn't really gain momentum until I developed trusting relationships.

So, what kind of challenges that could occur during a real estate transaction do you help clients avoid?

Justine González: At the beginning of your journey, this can be really overwhelming and intimidating. This is especially true if you don't have any prior knowledge and you are brand new to real estate investing. During this time, it is vital to have someone that you trust in your corner; you need someone that is going to be transparent with you, and if you don't have that, what I found is, that is when the learning process is most often abandoned.

I think that anytime we start to move forward with an investment, we want to know exactly what we're getting into, especially when we are women that are new to real estate investing. This is where I think mentors can help because you need that voice of reason, someone who has been through the process and will help you focus your plan of action. It also tends to give women a safe place where they can ask questions and not feel as if they are getting taken advantage of. I will say that if you don't have anybody to answer your questions and be a guide, then it'll be very tough to be successful.

Why do you think it's important for someone who's first embarking on this to get a real estate investment coach and sit down to talk to them before they go out on their own?

Justine González: I always say that if you fail to plan, then you plan to fail.

In my time working with launching schools and turnaround efforts, I have realized that one of the biggest predictors of your success is writing it down and making it plain—and then having someone holding you accountable to it. You need someone that is experienced, that will help you through the tough times but cheer you on through your victories. This is what I provide by having a succinct process with actions that can be practiced during the coaching. I wish there would have been this type of coaching when I first got interested in real estate over ten years ago because I feel like I would be in a completely different place now.

What challenges do you help new real estate investors avoid?

Justine González: One of the biggest things I help new real estate investors avoid is just jumping into the transaction. If you don't know how to set up a relationship, or leverage those relationships and sustain them, at some point, you'll be disappointed, or maybe someone that you work with will be disappointed. I think that this is one of the biggest things that I can help new investors avoid: walking away from real estate investing or not being equipped with the tools needed to be involved in the right type of deal for them and what they truly want and desire.

One of the biggest things that I can help people avoid is going in blindly without a plan and without an understanding of how to build those foundational relationships that will give you longevity in building your next real estate investment.

How can real estate investing make someone's life easier or better?

Justine González: Real estate investing gives you a lot of options as far as freedom; the most attractive thing for me was the freedom that it offers and realizing that I could have my money working for me in very different ways than what it was. This is about creating a second career or passive income while you still have your other career, and I think that's most newcomers' story, the driving force for them.

When I first started teaching, I was twenty-one, and our school had this assigned financial advisor from some large company. At that time, I knew that I had big goals but didn't really have a plan on how to get there. So, when I sat down with the advisor, we started talking about how much I could put away for retirement. He asked when I wanted to retire, and I told him by the time I was 45. After that, though, he laughed at me, and I just kind of sat there until he realized that I was serious.

I share this because there are often only a few options for retirement, and you just trust that you'll receive your pension. I realized that I really didn't know a whole lot at all, and this can be incredibly scary, but this is kind of what led me to start with what I do for our newcomer investors. It's even understanding what you are working with; I have found that a lot of professionals are doing well and have been successful, but they don't have a clue what they're set to retire with.

Can you share a success story about someone that you've helped either through a goal that they have reached or anything exciting that has happened to them?

Justine González: There's a woman who I know very well—she and her spouse both make above average income, and she has always been interested in investing in real estate. She was a client, so we were going through simple questions about how she will tap into her savings or retirement investing. She didn't know how much she had in retirement, and on top of that, she didn't even know how to access her retirement account. So, this is a lifelong educator and wants to be set to retire in the next five years. Right now, she is in her fifties, and to see how far she has come, it's been incredible.

The process is helping her realize her dream. The coaching and learning process, as well, has helped her zero in on what's important in her retirement journey. Now, she feels an urgency and excitement in her life because she doesn't just have a vague plan for 'someday'— she wants to make this happen soon rather than later.

What inspired you to become a real estate coach?

Justine González: Well, I really started getting serious about real estate investing when I met Monick, the lead author on the project. She has been so helpful as a mentor, and I realized that I could only get as far as who I was learning from. I wasn't her typical client, but she never gave up on me; it connected us, and I still consider her a mentor and friend.

Honestly, I'm forever grateful that she was willing to help build a relationship and to help me achieve my dreams. When you're coming over into this world from a different sector, it can also be intimidating. The reason is that you might feel as though real estate people or finance people are all focused on the bottom line, and that might be true sometimes, but I think Monick stood out as something different. Despite her network, she really valued me as a person; I clicked with her better. I think if we can coach people to do the same, then it's just a win-win for all parties involved when you're moving forward.

Is there a lesson that you learned early on in real estate that stuck with you today and made you a better or stronger investor?

Justine González: I believe that you go through different phases in your journey, but I think that always going back to the core is what matters most. For me, that's the relationship; it's about having a conversation and helping people achieve what they really want.

I think that my greatest word of wisdom would be to lean into your strengths and those things that you're still growing in. Make sure that you build relationships with people who are way better at those things.

What is the most important question that women should ask themselves about where they are, where they want to be, and what they need to do to reach those goals?

Justine González: I think she needs to ask herself *why* she is interested in real estate investing. Why does she want to get into real estate investing, and why does she want something different for her finances? You must start by asking yourself why, since you are the only person that can understand and hold that.

What are three reasons a relationship coach is important to a real estate transaction?

Justine González: Number one, it will help you find value in the process. Number two, it will help you act responsibly and relationally. Third, it will help you develop and be held accountable for your own plan of action.

What would you say to a woman who is interested in real estate investing and is thinking about getting started?

Justine González: I would say that you must take it one step at a time. Start with building your foundation, building your why. The best way to take it one step at a time, though, is to have the right coach— one who is encouraging and will also hold you accountable for those goals. You need to build relationships and a support system on those relationships.

Where can those that are interested in you, your company, and real estate investing get into contact with you?

Justine González: The best way would be through our business website: GraysonGonzalez.com. You can also find out more about me and connect with me through LinkedIn.

About Justine González

Company: Grayson and Gonzalez

Who I can help: Women who are new to real estate investing or trying to build their portfolio. I believe that you deserve to have a partner while you learn and grow in your journey toward building wealth through real estate investing.

What sets me apart: My company, Grayson and Gonzalez, was founded by women *for* women. We even have a new program we've designed specifically for new investors who may be starting out with smaller amounts of capital called *Portfolio Builders*. We understand the barriers to break into real estate investing are often related to the capital you have available. We are able to get you started despite those challenges.

Testimonial: "What you're doing is amazing! You can't imagine what a blessing you are in my life." – Current client and K12 school consultant

How to get in touch with me:
Email: justine.r.gonzalez@gmail.com
Website: GraysonGonzalez.com

Social Media:
LinkedIn.com/in/JustineGonzálezLeadership

Scan here to learn more:

A 'Must Have' Partner You Need for any Real Estate

One of the most important members of your real estate investment team is your CPA. Before you consider any real estate investments, you should discuss your strategy with an accountant to ensure that you have a solid tax plan. Does the idea of taxes make your head spin? Are you hesitant to invest because real estate investments will cause a giant nightmare at tax time? Marie Grasmeier knows exactly how you feel, and she's here to assist throughout the process and will help you get maximum returns on your investments. As a Certified Public Accountant for nearly two decades, Marie has unique skills and experience that allow her to understand the ways that real estate investing enhances an individual's overall portfolio. As the owner of her own CPA firm, Marie works with clients across the globe, helping everyday people, just like you, structure and implement sound real estate investment plans. With a specialty in complex real estate strategies, she is qualified in the area and enjoys working with novice and highly sophisticated investors.

Conversation with Marie Grasmeier

So, Marie, what do you do, and how do you help women invest in real estate?

Marie Grasmeier: My company is Grasmeier Business Consulting, and it is a tax and accounting firm, but in addition to traditional CPA services, we also provide Management Accounting Services and Business Consulting. Traditionally, tax practices focus on external reporting and compliance. However, in a consulting capacity, I help my real estate investors find the right vehicle for their investments to achieve the returns that they are looking for. I'm also proactively planning for potential tax issues that may arise in the future. A lot of my clients are professionals who may not have the time to manage a portfolio themselves; so, for them, a passive investment such as a Real Estate Investment Trust or a Syndication may be a great option.

Why do you think that real estate investing is beneficial to women?

Marie Grasmeier: I think that it's important for women to oversee their own finances and to be financially secure, no matter what happens in life. Investing in real estate provides many tax benefits, often generates steady cash flow and creates financial independence.

What kind of challenges or potential problems do you help investors avoid during a real estate transaction?

Marie Grasmeier: I have many international clients, and some are not aware that when a non-US person disposes of US Real Property, the transaction is subject to withholding tax under the Foreign Investment in Real Property Tax Act. This withholding is usually 15% of the gross sales price and is directly deducted from the sales proceeds at closing unless there is an exception from withholding or the seller has applied for a Withholding Certificate. This can be a big surprise at the closing table if the seller is not advised properly. The 15% of gross proceeds does not consider the actual tax liability and is often significantly higher than the actual capital gains tax on the net gain. I try to educate my clients about this provision so they can properly plan for this in advance.

Another challenge is the timing of gain recognition for a taxpayer disposing of capital gain property. Again, with proper planning, I can help with a like-kind exchange where the proceeds are used to acquire a replacement property; we can do advanced planning for the timing of capital losses or direct the funds into a deferral vehicle such as an Opportunity Fund.

I also help clients with the due diligence process when it comes to purchasing and selling real estate. It's important to look at the cash flows and cap rate, find out what the owner benefits are and ensure that there are no pending liens or other issues that the client should be aware of.

Why do you think it's important for someone just getting into the real estate game to work with a CPA, especially when starting out?

Marie Grasmeier: I think it is not just needed but crucial to work with a CPA. A professional can help analyze all the aspects of the investment. I meet with new clients without a charge, and if they leave thinking that they are better off on their own, then that is perfectly fine. There are many things to consider when you get into an investment—especially since it may involve putting down a big chunk of savings and taking away discretionary monthly cash flow. I also think that it's important to work with a client's team of advisors, including—but not limited to—attorneys, insurance agents, and financial advisors. It is always good to have a professional team to look at the overall picture and provide guidance along the way.

What kind of challenges would you say real estate investing eliminates for someone? How could investing help solve or improve someone's life?

Marie Grasmeier: I would say that real estate investing can improve many aspects of a person's life. It can provide peace of mind about retirement, generate supplemental income and build wealth. With monthly cash flow from an investment, debt can be paid off, and new investments can be made. Interest on real estate loans is deductible, and so are taxes and any rental-related expenses. When factoring in depreciation expense, oftentimes a person will have a loss for tax purposes, even if there is positive cash flow from the investment.

Can you share a success story?

Marie Grasmeier: I have a successful client from overseas, whom I admire very much. When she first came here, she was married, and her husband ran a start-up business. However, they ended up getting a divorce; she bought out her husband and started a new life from scratch. With some smart investing, she was able to secure investment properties and grew the business. She's now an avid investor and is doing fantastic owning properties and businesses globally; it's just a great success story!

What would you say inspired you to become a CPA and become involved in real estate in particular?

Marie Grasmeier: I was born in South Korea but raised in Sweden. During high school, I had the opportunity to study abroad for a year, and I finished my senior year in high school in Maryland. I had plans to eventually go into the medical field but decided to take a leap year and returned to the U.S. While I was here, I met my husband, who at the time was in property management, and he suggested that I go into accounting to help with taxes and bookkeeping.

Accounting wasn't necessarily more interesting than anything else, but I really liked the accounting classes, and now I love that I can help people daily. A lot of people are scared about taxes, they're afraid of the IRS, and they procrastinate with their tax filings. I try to make the process a pleasant experience, and I'm here to show my clients that there's nothing to be afraid of.

What is an important lesson that you learned early on as a CPA that made you a stronger CPA to work with now?

Marie Grasmeier: I have learned that integrity and competence are equally important to be a competitive CPA.

We all make mistakes, and the first few are horrible because you don't know how to best handle the situation or how to tell a client that you've made a mistake. The important lesson is that you must own it and you must learn from it. Once you've done that, it doesn't matter if the client is upset or if they leave you because, at least, you took the high road. I think that's part of what distinguishes a good, objective and trustworthy CPA.

When women are looking at getting into investing in real estate, what is the most important thing for them to consider or ask?

Marie Grasmeier: I think that the perfect place to start is by looking at the personal financial statement. This will show where the assets and liabilities are and what the cash flow and investable income look like.

The second thing to consider is what you will need to retire and how to get there. As a CPA, I will look at future cash flows and identify how it needs to grow to meet retirement goals.

Lastly, I advise women to create a strategic plan, find a team of advisors that will help implement it and follow up regularly until the goals are accomplished.

When it comes to real estate, there are many options, and the strategic plans often involve a direct personal real estate investment or pooling funds with friends and family.

What are three qualities that someone should look for when choosing a CPA to work with?

Marie Grasmeier: I think that the three important qualities to look for in a CPA are competence, integrity, and relatability. A competent CPA will have the proper licenses in place, a bachelor's degree in accounting, master's degree in accounting or tax and may also have other professional designations.

We discussed integrity earlier, and a CPA should be objective, free from conflicts of interest, and honest. Each State has a public record of licensed CPAs where any complaints against him or her will be listed. You can see how long the CPA has been licensed in the State as well.

When working with women, I think relatability is very important. I try to communicate tax codes and regulations so it makes sense to someone without an accounting background or to someone whose first language is not English. I think that it's important to feel comfortable with your CPA because it will build trust and pave the way for a long-term relationship.

What would you say to a woman interested in real estate investing? What would you want her to know?

Marie Grasmeier: I first would say, "Absolutely do it." There are no drawbacks that I can think of if you do it the right way and you have professionals to assist you. I would say, "Let's talk; let's find out what you're interested in, what your goals are, and come up with a plan."

How can customers get into touch with you?

Marie Grasmeier: My website is MarieCPA.com; all my information is on my website.

About Marie Grasmeier

Company: Grasmeier Business Consulting

Who I can help: I can help a woman wanting to invest in real estate from the initial conceptual process of identifying investment options to the very end in selecting an optimal exit strategy and planning for the tax consequences.

What sets me apart: I listen to my clients' needs and try to understand what they are looking for. I love connecting people and often introduce my clients to each other where I see a mutually beneficial relationship. I work with realtors, brokers, developers, property managers, and companies in all kinds of service industries, so there are a lot of synergies. I truly care about my clients, and their success is my success!

How to get in touch with you:
Email: marie@mariecpa.com
Website: MarieCPA.com

Social Media:
LinkedIn.com/in/Marie-Grasmeier-4681351

Scan here to learn more:

Why Land is Better than Houses! Live Your Dreams Investing in a Hidden Gem You see Every Day

Flipping houses and investing in real estate are sure-fire ways to make passive income. But when you think about property, have you ever considered land? That's right! Not houses, mobile homes, apartment buildings, or commercial structures; just good old-fashioned land. Land could be the most overlooked asset class in real estate. Think about it; vacant land is everywhere, yet how many people do you know who focus on it? If you've never thought about investing in land, then wait until you hear from land investment expert Michelle Bosch. Michelle is a seasoned land investor with over 4,000 real estate transactions under her belt. She's been both producing cash and cash flow since 2002 and helping investors with land flipping since 2008, and she owns multiple businesses: an educational company in partnership with her husband as well as an investment firm.

Over the years, she has also expanded into additional areas and now also syndicates the purchase of larger 100+ apartment buildings and actively manages them to top performance. With her vast experience, Michelle is, therefore, an ideal syndicator to work with for new and seasoned investors. After leaving a demanding job to become a full-time real estate investor, Michelle credits her decision to focus on real estate investing on the desire to living the life she always dreamed of. Her insight will show you the steps to obtain the life you're dreaming of right now.

Conversation with Michelle Bosch

So, tell us about your company, what the focus of the company is, and what kind of problems you solve.

Michelle Bosch: My husband, Jack, and I started our real estate investing company in 2002, so we have been in business for many years now.

We are both immigrants to the United States. We came with absolutely nothing and started from scratch. Originally, we first started looking into houses but didn't know anything about it. We didn't know where to get the money to buy these properties, how to estimate repairs, how to even know what needed to be repaired and what not ... Then we stumbled into land and realized how easy it was to pretty much flip a piece of land and get either the same or better profit than we would have if we had gotten into houses. You don't need to deal with tenants, toilettes, termites, repairs, mold, contractors, banks, inspectors, and you don't even need to go see the land (what is there to see—trees?); plus, you can do it without much competition, make great profits (often better than houses with much less hassles) and even make land cash flow. Yes, you read that right.

Now, we have completed over 4,000 deals, which ends up being about $40 million in real estate that we have bought and sold over the years. In 2008, we started investing for buy and hold in the single-family residential space, and in 2016, we decided to start syndicating and investing in multifamily apartment buildings and currently have $30 million in assets under management. So, it has been a fun and exciting journey.

Investing in land is beautifully simple because it's real estate without houses—and because you don't have to worry about rehabbing a house, or mortgages, or tenants ... you don't have to even have experience to start. As a result, our students are incredibly successful in a world where most other investors are complaining about competition.

And since 2008, we have taken people to their first checks of $9,000, $15,000, or even $75,000 … They are literally being reported daily. I don't think that people who flip houses get those kinds of results, and it goes back, again, to how simple land flipping is.

What kind of return on investment (ROI) do your projects typically offer? What is the full range of investment opportunities that you provide to clients?

Michelle Bosch: In our land business we don't offer any ROIs; we teach people how they can do their own deals. But their results speak for themselves, and ROIs of 50% to as much as 1,000% (no kidding) when selling a property for 10 times what you bought it for are not uncommon. We just focus on our own deals, and in addition, we offer a home study course, support, and also coaching so that our students can stand on their own two feet within a short time.

Why do you think investing in real estate is advantageous to women in particular?

Michelle Bosch: This land investment strategy is perfect for women. Land deals pay the same, no matter who does the deals. Our system allows for major flexibility in time. Because there is so little competition in this space, you, for example, can make offers when YOU HAVE TIME, which is important particularly for women who wear all hats (and don't we all?). It's also a great way for women to show their kids that they don't have to rely on a man, and it further allows one to truly work on leaving a legacy.

What are some common fears that you see women have when investing in real estate?

Michelle Bosch: I think one of the biggest concerns I've seen would be not knowing anything about real estate or thinking that they don't have a lot of money. So, their holdup is really a matter of knowledge and money. Yet, as mentioned before, because land doesn't have walls, plumbing, repairs, mold, toilettes, or roofs which need to be inspected, and because we can buy some properties for under $1,000, anyone can do this, even without experience, and with very little money. Plus, you can outsource most pieces of this business without it costing much at all, and you can run a 6- or even 7-figure business pretty much from your living room and in your spare time. But that leaves an issue that really underlies all those mentioned above, and that is CONFIDENCE: It's not money or knowledge people are missing; it's confidence.

In my company, we walk you through a process called 'The Four Cs': **commitment, courage, capability, and confidence.** As you go through a full land flipping cycle, you also pass through these 4 phases of: 1. having to commit to the goal; 2. building the courage to do it; 3. getting the capability by actually doing it; and 4. building the confidence in yourself and in your skills by having done a deal. After you complete your first few deals, you have confidence and faith in your yourself. This starts growing your faith in the goodness of others, the unknown, everything. So, in addition to building wealth, real estate investments (and in particular, land flips) can sculpt your spirit and take you from an outlook that the world is out to get you to an outlook that everyone is supporting you.

What do you feel are some of the biggest myths that people have when they come into real estate investing?

Michelle Bosch: I think that one of the biggest myths is that they don't have the money to invest. Like I mentioned, there are so many ways that you can structure a deal, so you don't have to have the money up front.

I think another one of the biggest myths is that you must have money to make money. To some extent, yes, this is correct in that even to find your seller, you're going to have to spend some time and a little bit of money on marketing, but that requires no more than a few hundred dollars, not thousands of dollars. People think that they need tens of thousands or hundreds of thousands plus great credit to be able to invest, but we are talking about land that you can buy very cheap and then flip for a very nice profit without ever having to talk to a bank or borrowing even $1.

Another myth is that people think land doesn't cash flow—yet we have done it thousands of times using a process called SELLER FINANCING, aka Installment Sale. When selling with seller financing, the buyer gives you a down payment, and then they make monthly payments (just like you buy your own house; just that you are now the BANK). So, you get cash flow without tenants, toilettes, and termites.

Another thing that we tend to hear from people is that they don't have a lot of time. However, what we teach our clients is that they can outsource a lot of the core pieces of the process and just focus on the key activities, which are buying and selling the property. If you have a bit of time for that, everything else can be outsourced, even the marketing.

Particularly, after the market crash in 2008, what would you say to someone who is worried about investing in real estate?

Michelle Bosch: One of the biggest things that I hear from different people is that they have a misconception that real estate is risky. However, I think what happens is that people don't understand that in different stages of the market, you can make money.

Personally, I feel almost like investing is not really risky: the PEOPLE investing are risky because they might not understand the strategies that they should use based on the market cycle. This is a matter of educating yourself in the market and figuring out what strategies are going to be best to up your market.

For example, right now, there are a lot of buyers in the market, which is great. This means that the strategy of quick flips is going to be incredibly relevant right now and is also useful for making money. So, during different stages of the marketing cycle, you might be focusing on different types of investments. Right now, for instance, you should look at quick flips, or invest in quick flips, rather.

How does real estate investing make life better?

Michelle Bosch: I am going to talk as a mother, a wife, a woman and a business owner here.

So, you know that I have confidence because I have sixteen years of experience under my belt, I know I am able to generate a large check. I know that I can do it.

I think that some women might not have that confidence, and real estate is a great builder of confidence in life (and provides a great income); either they have never been in this, or the husband has been taking care of it, whatever. So, no matter if you are married or if you're a single woman, you need to go out there and do this on your own and have the confidence that you can provide for your family.

You can then use this money to perhaps change things around to dedicate more time to your children because, particularly, our real estate model can be molded to fit your lifestyle. With real estate investing, you can have your business fit your lifestyle.

Really, the benefits are multi-fold, and there are so many things that real estate can provide, and you can really help in making your life better. And then, if you think about it from a legacy standpoint, you can build something for your kids, for this generation, or even generations to come.

How can you help women find and achieve success through real estate investing?

Michelle Bosch: For me, everything that I do is a matter of the heart, even if it includes something like hard cash—like real estate investing does. I'm doing these things for a reason, and it's to give our clients the confidence to go and create financial freedom for themselves. And that is why we teach this. We have courses, coaching, software, and events to help our students succeed, but at the end, I care about the people that I work with, and it's a matter of the heart for us to help them.

What are some tips and tricks you can give to women that are just starting out in their real estate investment journey?

Michelle Bosch: First, I'd say don't try it without guidance. My husband and I started our business sixteen years ago, and it took us three years to find out alone how to do this. Once we figured this out, though, within eighteen months, we were millionaires.

I would also say in addition to analyzing the strategy, you also want to really study who you are getting ready to commit to learning from. Focus on the who: who are you doing this for; who is going to help you; who are you bringing along to make your dreams come true. Make sure that the person you have aligned with is going to have a transformational—not transitional—relationship with you. There's a lot of people in the real estate industry that do not have their student's best interest in mind—that's not to say that it's everyone, but it's just what it is.

What inspired you to start working in real estate?

Michelle Bosch: So, both my husband and I are immigrants into the U.S. I, from Honduras, and he, from Germany. My mom was a single mother—my father passed away when I was very young. She was a teacher, but my dad had bought a piece of real estate to supplement her income, and that asset ended up allowing her to provide a great education for me. She was able to send me to a private school where I was able to learn English.

My mom had faith in me, as did my dad, and that one great decision of buying that property allowed her the freedom to give me the best that she could. Otherwise, I wouldn't be able to communicate with you in English right now or even be able to come to the U.S. to study. I have a degree in Finance, then an MBA, and that cost was absorbed by that piece of real estate.

When we first moved here, Jack was a business analyst for a technology company, and I was an analyst for Motorola. We hated these jobs and were traveling all week, but we needed them for our work permit and green cards. After a few years, we got so fed up with our current situation that we looked around and found real estate out of sheer dissatisfaction with our lives.

When we stumbled into this, we did this slowly, and we couldn't leave our jobs—because we needed employer dependent work visa to stay in the USA.

Now, though, we have a passive income that allows us to take three to four months off per year. Last year, we homeschooled our daughter for six months while traveling the world. We also have an amazing investment team, a property management team, an educational team, all of which are aligned with our values, and of course long-lasting cash flow (Forever Cash). Real estate made it possible. And I love that it can be wherever you want to be, and you don't even have to live close to the land you flip.

What are some lessons you learned early on that make you feel like you are a better investor today?

Michelle Bosch: I think that the biggest mistake we made at first was being rugged individualists: we wanted to do everything by ourselves.

The moment that we started expanding and thinking of blessing others, bringing a team in to help us gave us an incredible amount of freedom and ease. So, what I would say to reiterate what I said earlier: don't do it alone. Think of who is coming with you and be mindful of the relationships that fuel you. Don't be an individualist and think that you can do this all alone—we all need each other.

What three qualities do you recommend for a woman starting their real estate investment journey when looking for a real estate investor to work with?

Michelle Bosch: First, I think that transparency is important. It's important to see how the person you work with operates, and transparency is key.

Integrity is next: you need to be sure that the person you are working with will do the right thing, even if it's hard sometimes. You need to be sure that they are going to do what they said that they are going to do.

Transformational relationships are the last thing. These relationships should be built with your best interests in mind now and in the future, not just for the time being to make a buck. You want to create a relationship that goes beyond this one deal or this one transaction: you want someone that is willing to support you long term.

I think that those are the three things that come to mind. I look at every idea, project, or opportunity through a filter: one of transparency, integrity, and transformation. This gives you an opportunity to filter out the projects that might not work with you and find the best ones that will help you evolve into who you were meant to be.

What is the most important question that a woman should ask herself when thinking about where she is today, where she wants to be tomorrow, and how she can get there?

Michelle Bosch: I like to say that we have limited time on this earth. I always think of what I'm spending my time on now and aligning this with ambitions and learning. So, if you're looking at ways to bridge that gap between where you are and where you want to go, you should have a clear understanding as to where you want to be.

If you met someone who said that they didn't have time or energy to work with real estate investments, what would you say to that person to tell them that they should still pursue this?

Michelle Bosch: I think if the person is already making six figures and loves what they're doing, that is fine; they should keep going the same way and, instead, just consider investing passively for cash flow. But for those who say they don't love what they do, and they don't have the time or energy, there are multiple ways that we can fix that. We work with people in all kinds of life situations and help them get to make money either passively by investing in our syndications or actively through a mostly outsourced land flipping business.

Can you share a success story of someone you have worked with previously?

Michelle Bosch: Renee would be one. She was able to generate $500,000 in cash on the side—just from investing in land and not leaving her job. She has pretty much outsourced everything. She just retired in February from her 'day job' and is now doing this full-time. And she is only one of 100s, if not 1000s, who have found success with our program.

How can someone interested in real estate get in touch with you?

Michelle Bosch: If you want to learn about our course, you can visit LandProfitGenerator.com. You can also join our Facebook community for free, called The Forever Cash Club, at Facebook.com/groups/ForeverCashClub/. Once there, you can see deals happening on a daily basis and be part of all the conversations.

About Michelle Bosch

Company:

Orbit Investments, LLC.

Who I can help: We work with women entrepreneurs, as well as mothers, to help them generate a second income while also promoting the ideas of confidence and financial freedom.

Michelle Bosch is a mother and real estate land investor and consultant. She travels the world, teaching courses in how to make real estate profitable as well as how to use it to achieve financial goals. In addition, Michelle and her husband, Jack, through their company, have done over 4,000 real estate deals, worth $40,000,000. Also, the two have written an Amazon best-selling book about financial philosophy, called *Forever Cash*.

What sets me apart: I help women not only with the Outer Work of making money but also with the Inner Work of having faith in themselves so they can go on to do their 'Higher Work.'

Testimonial: "It has been an incredible Asia vacation. In the last 16 days, we have closed 3 separate deals, netting us profit of $32,682.88!! Another netted us $12,146.39, and the last $8,000. Without Michelle and Jack's system, none of this would have been possible."–Kittikanda Kukkai and Justin Harris

How to get in touch with me:
Email: michelle@orbitinvestments.com
Website: LandProfitGenerator.com

Social Media:
Facebook.com/ForeverCashClub

Scan here to learn more:

Rehab, Renovate, & Restore Homes While Doing the Same in Your Own Life

Would you like to make money in real estate while rebuilding your own life? What if you could participate in a real estate investment opportunity where you renovate homes and renovate yourself at the same time from the inside out? Highly successful contractor Kimle Nailer can help you build wealth through construction. She specializes in helping women transform houses that look like they should be demolished into livable homes while doing the same for you in your own life. Are you concerned about the costs or skills required to flip a home? Kimle has assisted clients in flipping homes, renovating, and buying and holding, with a special focus on the goldmine of Detroit real estate. With a builder's license to invest all around the country and years of success, Kimle is your investment partner to start rehabbing, renovating, and restoring homes. Kimle can help you find the capital to start not only rehabbing homes but rehabbing your life too. Her tagline is: "We build structures, and We build Lives."

Conversation with Kimle Nailer

Tell us a little bit about your company, your program for women, and why investing in residential projects for rehab, renovation, and restoration can change and positively impact a woman's life.

Kimle: Nail-Rite Construction is 100% woman-owned and has been established since 1995. We provide residential and commercial construction services. I have been renovating homes for investors, including myself, since that time. One of the things we offer is training in the skilled trades so women understand the opportunities that exist. We also help people to look at their current financial state and show them how to leverage real estate purchases to achieve and build wealth. We can help you identify your immediate needs and identify the fastest ways to elevate your wealth and reposition yourself financially.

Can you share a little bit about what types of investment opportunities you offer and how much is required for the initial investment?

Kimle: We offer one of three investments: Someone looking for extra cash flow (rental properties), somebody who wants to just build their portfolio of having more assets and building an equity stake (buy and hold property), and then there are the people who just want immediate cash (flip and sell). It's based on what your initial needs are, and you can invest based on the outcome you're looking for. We have some low entry points, but if you're looking for some equity positions, you may use as much as $50,000 to $60,000.

How long does it take to recoup an investment?

Kimle: Again, that depends on the type of investment you're making. So, let's say you are flipping a home. We're going to buy a house this month, take two or three months to get it fixed up on the market and then sell it. So, immediately, you're going to get a return on your investment, maybe $5,000 to $10,000, just based on what you found. The day you sell, and you may have put in $15,000, and you sell it for $25,000, you just immediately made $10,000 on your $15,000 investment. Or it might be a situation where you say, "You know what? I want to hold this property because I see the market is changing." The $25,000 can grow to $50,000 or more.

Why is investing in real estate advantageous for women?

Kimle: One of the key reasons is that most of our working years, we're earning less than our male counterparts. And if you're a black woman, it could be even more of a gap. So, if you don't have an opportunity to earn the same amount of money over your living years when you actually have those expenses, how are you going to actually save for your wealth creation, for your retirement years? It's very advantageous to use the real estate asset medium whereby you can use property value to safely get a return on your investment with some predictability. There's always a risk in anything we do, but with real estate, I always make money on paper before I ever close on a deal and start the process, so I know exactly how much I'm going to make it.

I don't know of any other investment that allows that much predictability. I mean, most of these women are working and may be moms; they may have families, and they don't want to risk too much. With real estate, you can actually calculate your risk clearly on paper, make the investment and put the money in your pocket.

What is the benefit of working with you as a residential home and commercial contractor?

Kimle: Not only am I a licensed builder that's skilled and talented, but I am also a real estate investor. So, my prospective of the project that I'm awarded is seen through the lens of a real estate investor who wants to make money and make their money quickly. I know the type of investments to make to improve property value for sale and when to put emphasis on the kitchen or bath. I can also help you not over-invest in the property that you're going to be getting the cash flow from when you buy and hold.

What are the biggest myths when it comes to investing in real estate?

Kimle: I think a lot of people think real estate investing is for wealthy people, and they think you have to have a lot of money or you can't do it while working. What I like to tell people is that every year, most people get a tax return—just save a couple of tax returns and get started.

You can partner with someone who can lead you through the process and answer any questions you have. A lot of people have concerns about their credit. When I started real estate, my credit was raunchy. I bought some properties using credit cards. My first purchase was with the Discover card, and it started immediate cash flow. I would use one credit card to buy it, another credit card to make the improvements, and then sell the property and make money.

Wow. Okay. Any other myths that bubble up for you?

Kimle: A lot of people think it's going to take a long time. As I shared with you, many of these processes are two to three months; so, in the course of a year, you can really reposition yourself in an amazing way. Some companies or some states require a longer seasoning process, which means the length of time you've owned the property before you could actually borrow against that property. With one project completed in three to four months maximum, you have increased your net worth, improved your cash flow or just made a lump sum if you had an immediate sale. You can really change your financial position using real estate.

What are some misconceptions around the real estate industry, especially since the 2008 market crash, that are not true today? And why is now a good time to invest?

Kimle: Well, a lot of people feel that you may not build any equity in property anymore, so people are afraid to invest. I like to tell people it can happen again, true, because nothing is predictable. But when you're making your investment, you're basing it on what's happening right now. You just target those areas where property value is rising, so it's always a great opportunity to invest in real estate somewhere. A real estate agent or a real estate investor can help you find those key areas. Detroit right now is a very hot spot. There are people coming from around the nation and around the globe to invest in this city because it's a great place where the appreciation is rising after the crash.

What are some of the most common fears that you found that women have about getting started in real estate investing?

Kimle: A lot of women are just not comfortable with risking large sums of money because, in real estate, you're talking $5,000, $10,000 or $15,000 per transaction. When you bought your home, if you're buying a home, you made a down payment, and you make monthly payments. You can use the exact same process in real estate investing. You don't have to offer a cash deal either. Put down a deposit and make monthly payments. The person renting from you is making those monthly payments, but you're adding to your wealth by creating a bigger portfolio of properties, so you don't have to worry about losing money. Someone can pay that down payment for you also. You might pay the down payment initially, but the first and last months' security deposit from the tenant became the down payment to purchase the house.

There are other people who say: "I just don't know enough about real estate." There's a lot of books that you can read, and with HGTV today, you can learn how to start making improvements and flipping houses. Thank God we have Google and YouTube to also learn what to do. A good broker and real estate investor can really eliminate all those common concerns that you have around the fear of losing money. You can lose money in anything you do.

What are some other ways that real estate investing can make life better?

Kimle: You have immediate access to adequate cash flow if that's what you need. It can help you pay down debt and reposition yourself financially. If you're looking to just put large sums into your nest egg for your retirement, with a couple of transactions buying, selling, and flipping, you can get a $10,000 or $15,000 increase that you may not be able to save over the course of the year otherwise. You want to take a nice dream vacation, you can pull money out of one of your investment properties and go take that $3,000 or $4,000 trip leveraging rental properties.

What's some advice if you encounter people who don't believe they have access to the capital?

Kimle: Well, that's common because anytime you go into business, you need access to capital; it can be the number one challenge. In the real estate market, they have a system that is called wholesaling, or some people call it bird-dogging. How it works is, you might find a vacant home that you can research to find out if it is a city-owned property or abandoned property. You can get the address and advertise, "Is there an investor in the area looking to buy homes?" An investor may be glad to say, "Here's some money for helping me locate a deal." Then they can go ahead and complete the transaction with the city or the broker, but you've made some money just by locating an opportunity for an investor. You do that a couple of times, and you have money to get into the game yourself.

How can you help a woman who is interested in real estate investing achieve her greatest success?

Kimle: Well, one of the things we would do initially is just really find out what it is they want to do. What is the real goal? Are they looking for money? Once we know what the real story is, that's where we will develop the best strategy for them to have success. Maybe the goal is to just get access to more money. Then I would recommend they buy and sell a property, and I would make sure they're successful with the transaction. Now, if they continue, they're accumulating money to achieve their success. They now have more money in their accounts and larger portfolios. With a self-directed Roth IRA, they can also manage their money and the growth, and that's what real estate does.

Can you share a story about one of your investors and a success that they accomplished investing with you?

Kimle: So I recently helped a person purchase a home with about $20,000 worth of equity in it, and she bought it rehabbed already. She purchased with traditional home financing and was glad to have a new home. They were very excited. Well, guess what? That was a year or two before everything collapsed. So now, they have this home that maybe had 20 thousand dollars' worth of equity that now has just been diminished to a market value under $6,000 in a matter of 24 months. How would you feel about that? A first-time home buyer, you just made this big jump into the real estate market, and you're like, "Oh my God, I just lost everything." And so they decided to walk away because they didn't see the need to keep financing the property.

So, how do I help this client—I had just sold it as a great deal to become a homeowner with equity, and all of a sudden, that disappeared? So, I said, "Well, why don't you stay in one of my other properties and just pay rent there, and we'll get you situated?" I found another property for this woman, and the property had about $8,000 in back taxes, so she was able to make small monthly payments. Now she owns her house 100 percent clear and free. And with the appreciation of the market, she's now back to where she was, but she doesn't have a mortgage. She has a clear and free house, which is a better position than she was before.

She can now use her house as an asset to do some things that she may need to do. So, that's one of my biggest case studies.

What inspired you to become a contractor and residential specialist?

Kimle: I've been investing for many years, and I just got my builder's license in 2017, on the three-year anniversary of my mom's passing. Detroit is a very ripe market. During the downturn, people were coming in, buying properties in batches of 100, so I knew the market was going to change, and people are going to start renovating those homes. That inspired me to get my contractor's license because, now, I can work for these investors. I was excited because there's a lot of people who need to learn the trades of construction, and I'm in the commercial space, where there's a real shortage of trade skills. I use the residential properties to teach the skilled trades so they can go to the commercial properties for employment. I can teach drywall, painting, and some light electrical or mechanical skills, and how to operate with other trades in the same space. We're using these residential properties that we're helping investors get back on the market as a training platform for women to learn the trades. If you want to become a rehabber or flipper, and you know how to do the work yourself, now you can grow your portfolio while cutting some of that construction cost.

Could you share a lesson that you learned early on in this role of being a contractor/investor that makes you a more valuable real estate investor?

Kimle: Well, I think one of the lessons I've learned is to stay closely connected to the market and market trends and pay attention to what's being projected. There was a lot of projection about the real estate market, but I didn't pay close attention; I could have slowed my pace so if the market did change on me, I would have had fewer properties in need of being sold. In my last round of acquisition, I was just as aggressive buying and rehabbing homes, and I should've been paying a little more attention and maybe could have minimized my risk. The other lesson is learning skilled trades. When I first started investing, I was paying for everything to be done, and then I rolled up my sleeves and learned how to do some of the construction myself, and it saved some money on the front end so I could continue to grow faster. Now I can hire people again, so that's the thing you want to learn first—know when to let somebody else do it so you can get to the money quicker, or do it yourself if you need to save money. Also, knowing the trade allows you to better access the worker's quality of work.

What would you say is the most important question that women should ask themselves as they consider where they are today, where they want to be tomorrow, and how to plan to get there?

Kimle: I think the biggest question a woman should ask herself is, "What control do I have over my income?" "How much control do I have over my money?" "What is my retirement looking like? And what am I doing to preserve it? Am I hoping somebody else has that for me?" I think the number one question is, "Am I willing to risk somebody else controlling everything, or how much control do I want to have on my tomorrow?" The answers to these questions will help you decide how you want to play the game of real estate.

What would you say are three qualities a woman who's reading your chapter should consider when choosing a real estate investor to work with?

Kimle: You want to work with someone who has a good relationship and understanding of real estate, and they understand market trends and market values, so they can help you make good assessments.

Secondly, you also want to find someone who's willing to help you learn. They don't want to just do it all and keep you in the dark. They want to educate you.

Number three, work with someone who owns some property. I worked with someone who owned properties that could teach me and help me learn how to have more value in my property portfolio.

If you're evaluating a potential investor, what would be something that you could use as a metric of whether this person really gets it?

Kimle: Number one, do they own any property? How can they help you be a real estate investor if they don't own any property? Number two, do they have a portfolio of properties that they're managing? Then you can feel confident that person knows the game because they're actually doing it and not just telling you something that they read or watched on television. You want to see that quality in the person you choose to work with, and you want to know what experience they've had rehabbing if they're going to take you down to rehab path. I own a property, and I've been managing properties since '95.

For a woman who might say, "I'm already earning six figures" or "That sounds good, but I don't have the bandwidth to add anything else to my plate," why should she still consider adding real estate investing to her portfolio?

Kimle: Well, the woman should ask herself, "How much control do I have with that six-figure income?" You might be very busy and don't have much spare time, and that's why you want to partner with someone like myself who can help you manage investing in real estate. It's important to build a portfolio for your future needs that you control so you can still build the solidity of wealth and create an income that will be there for you. You don't want your six figures to stop when you stop working, when you could build a portfolio while working that has an equity value of a million dollars or more. So, when you decide to stop working a six-figure job that might be a little more stressful than you want to handle, you have a solid income to maintain that quality of life.

How can someone find out more about you and your real estate opportunities?

Kimle: You can reach me at area code 313-402-4997. Or you can reach me by email at knailer@nailrite.com, and I will gladly support you and your real estate investing efforts. I strongly encourage everyone to look in their neighborhood, their community, especially as women, and find areas where you can appreciate the value of your community and have an equity stake inside of it. Don't wait for investors to come into your neighborhood and buy up everything, and then you and the residents of your community are on the outside looking in or potentially pushed out of a neighborhood because the market is going so high. Just start with one property at a time, and we'll gladly support you.

About Kimle Nailer

Company:

Nail-Rite Construction Company, Inc

Who I can help: We work with investors seeking to develop single family or multi-unit housing, or who invest in commercial properties to improve stability in communities and inner-city neighborhoods.

Kimle Nailer is a licensed builder and a successful, heart-centered serial entrepreneur. She is the president and owner of Nail-Rite Construction, a women-owned business since 1995. She leveraged her corporate analyst background to also launch a real estate investment company, Fairport Investments, and also founded Positive S.I.S.T.E.R.S. to coach women in discovering their inner essence of beauty and strength to become prominent leaders. She is a dynamic Speaker, Best-Selling Author and Spiritual Intuitive Life Coach who uses her life's story of overcoming low self-esteem due to the dark color of her skin as a compelling message to help other women transition into confident, business women.

What sets me apart: As a licensed builder and investor, I help my clients analyze their rehab projects through the lens of an investor to maximize their ROI and quickly expedite their progress to access cash.

How to get in touch with me:
Email: knailer@nailrite.com
Website: NailRite.com

Social Media:
Twitter.com/kimlenailer

Scan here to learn more:

Financial Freedom for Women

Are you apprehensive about getting started in real estate investing? Have you ever heard of Non-Performing Notes? Buying non-performing loans or 'Notes' can be a very lucrative investment strategy. Non-performing notes are loans where the borrower is behind in their payments or has stopped making payments altogether. What makes non-performing notes so attractive to an investor is the opportunity to essentially purchase the asset at a discount, which builds in an equity cushion and mitigates risk.

With over 20 years of experience as a real estate investor, Paige Panzarello has a history of successfully investing in non-performing notes, and she applies her expertise to earn high ROI (return on investment) in her daily investment strategy. Paige was able to pay off her family estate's debt of $4 million in under three years, and now she's known as the Cashflow Chick for her ability to earn passive income and higher returns for herself and her clients with risk-averse investments. Read on to discover how Paige rebuilt her business after the devastating market crash of 2007 halted her, how she was able to not only turn things around but also obtain financial freedom, and how she can help you reach freedom you never imagined!

Conversation with Paige Panzarello

Paige, tell us about your company and why investing in first position non-performing notes secured by residential real estate can change and positively impact a woman's life.

Paige Panzarello: I'm known as the Cashflow Chick, and my company is The Tryllion Group. The Tryllion Group is a woman-owned business that specializes in non-performing notes. We also invest in self-storage, private lending, and multifamily investments, but our primary investment strategy is in non-performing notes. When you invest in non-performing notes, you literally become the bank. When you are the bank, there is a tremendous amount of control. When you have control, you can determine your own outcome and mitigate risk. This form of investing allows for the generation of chunks of cash and monthly cash flow in the same vehicle without the headaches of tenants and toilets. Note investing is not market dependent, nor is it location specific. I can do this business literally anywhere in the world as long as I have a phone and a computer.

Why is investing in real estate advantageous to women?

Paige Panzarello: Control and Freedom. We have a substantial amount of control over our future and our outcome. Real estate is all around us. We live in it, we work in it, we play in it, and we die in it. It's not a fad; it's a hard asset that secures your invested dollars. And it can also be protected by insurance. We create chunks of cash or streams of cash flow. We can invest passively, and that allows freedom—freedom to have the life we deserve both now and in the future. We can be creative and confident in our own decisions, and most millionaires are made through real estate investing.

What is the benefit of working with you as a non-performing notes specialist?

Paige Panzarello: This business is very reputation-based. I've developed connections over the years that our investors will benefit from, and I often receive private offerings or more significant discounts because my asset managers know that I do what I say I'm going to do. Also, being a woman-owned business, there are specific advantages that are not offered on the whole to other companies.

What do you feel are the biggest myths when it comes to investing in real estate (and your asset class)?

Paige Panzarello: Number one, especially for women, is that it's "beyond their ability." It always perplexes me because women can run households with kids and husbands and jobs and balance it all. But when it comes to investing, we feel inferior because this space has been dominated by men for so long. The second biggest myth is that you don't have the money—but there's money all around us. There are ways that you can work in a collaborative space, and if you can leverage other people's experience, you will have access to that money. I can teach you how to do that as well.

What are some common misconceptions around the real estate industry, especially since the 2008 market crash, that are not true today? Why is now a good time to invest in real estate?

Paige Panzarello: Most people think real estate will continue to go up, but that's not the case. If you look at history, the market corrects every 7–10 years, and we're already seeing signs of that correction happening right now. In my opinion, it's never a 'wrong time' to invest in real estate. You need to know the market cycle and choose a medium to invest in based on the current position of that market cycle. For instance, in a fix and flip market, you want to be careful not to overpay at the height of the market. That's why I love note investing so much. It's not dependent on the market cycle, and if there's a correction, we build in a big enough equity cushion that we will likely still have a profitable outcome.

What are some of the most common fears you have found that women have about getting started in real estate investing?

Paige Panzarello: "I'll lose money." "It's a man's industry." "I don't know about real estate." All of these unfounded fears, you can overcome. When we come together, and we work together, and we leverage each other's talents, there isn't anything that we can't do. Women can empower one another if they reach out to each other. So, if you have that 'collaboration versus competition' mindset, I truly believe you can overcome all of those fears and be very, very successful.

How can real estate investing make life better?

Paige Panzarello: The biggest benefit to any investor is freedom. If 'life happens' to you (divorce, loss of job, medical, death of a spouse, etc.), you have a backup plan. As a real estate investor, you're not dependent on an employer or a spouse for your well-being, or your ability to pay the bills, should something happen. You can build the life you want NOW and enjoy it, and you can build for the future. Most Americans that are 40+ years old don't have $25,000 saved for retirement, much less what they will need to have to live comfortably and without worry. That's a frightening statistic.

Paige, it sounds like real estate investing (and specifically non-performing notes) is something more women should consider as a revenue stream and a way to stop trading time for money. How can you help a woman who is interested in real estate investing achieve the greatest success?

Paige Panzarello: Successful people are successful *because* they've failed. You have the opportunity to leverage someone else's skinned knees, and we all have them. If you have that collaboration mindset, and you seek to invest with those that have that same mindset, you're going to be very successful.

I'm sure you've piqued some interest in what you've shared, but someone may be concerned as to where to find the money to invest in your projects if they don't believe they have access to capital. What is some advice you'd share with women who don't believe they have access to capital?

Paige Panzarello: It starts with talking to people around you about what you want to do and then developing those networks of people. Understand you are not asking for money. You are in a position to help others earn a better rate of return, and you will help yourself by having the capital to fund your investments by just talking about how you can collaborate together. Build a team behind you, around you, and underneath you that is going to help you to be successful. When using other people's money, you have to protect it better than you would protect your own money. It's a huge responsibility. But if you have that collaboration mindset and a team around you, you can safely raise the capital you need.

What is one problem you solve through real estate investing?

Paige Panzarello: Many people (especially women) are fearful of investing because they "don't know how" or are fearful they are going to lose money because they don't know the due diligence steps to take. I do know the steps to take, and I make the deal conform to us and our criteria, not the other way around. We have twenty-three different exit strategies that are available to us, and because of that, we can mitigate the risk of losing money. We're also in the unique position of helping people and families that have had life happen to them—a job loss, medical problems, divorce—and make money doing it. Lastly, I can help build a retirement that will support your golden years as opposed to being worried about how you are going to survive.

What types of investment opportunities do you offer?

Paige Panzarello: The best way to determine if we are a good fit is to schedule a call with me. Go to CashflowChick.com to book a free call with me.

What kind of return on investment (ROI) do your projects offer?

Paige Panzarello: Though there is never a guarantee of any specific return, we typically see higher than hard money lending returns, which means usually higher than 10–12%, with less risk.

What's the difference between working with you versus a competitor?

Paige Panzarello: There are undoubtedly other investing mediums that you can go into that may offer you higher returns, but there may be more risk involved. The Tryllion Group stands apart in that it employs several different investment strategies, as opposed to just a single strategy. The flexibility of having different strategies allows us to easily shift with the economy, market conditions, and opportunities as they are presented. Tryllion maintains an unyielding buying criterion based strictly on numbers and fact, not speculation or emotion. And that's how I protect your money.

Can you share a story about one of your investors and a success they accomplished investing with you?

Paige Panzarello: I have a JV partner who is a widow, and she was terrified of investing. She had $100,000 to her name. We spoke for about six months, and she finally made the decision that she wanted to invest all of it, and I refused. I refused all of the funds because I wanted her to have a safety net. We started with $50,000; we invested in a note that was five years behind in payments, and the note was secured by a very well-kept house in Tennessee.

It turned out our borrower's husband had died. She had two small children and lost her job, so the mortgage was severely in default and in the process of foreclosure.

We reduced her interest rate and her balance due by forgiving $30,000 of the arrearage that she owed and extended the term of her loan, which reduced her monthly payment to a manageable level. We required a small reinstatement fee which generated a chunk of cash for us. Then we cash-flowed the asset by collecting the monthly mortgage payments. Our borrower ended up writing us a beautiful letter thanking us for helping to save her home and keeping her kids safe and happy—it absolutely warmed our hearts. Now a performing note, after 12 months, we sold it to another investor. My JV partner came out 14 months later with a good return on investment, and her fear of investing has vanished. We literally created a win-win-win for everyone involved.

What inspired you to become a real estate investor and specialize in non-performing notes?

Paige Panzarello: I came into real estate investing by default. My grandmother had passed away, and we owned 38 townhome units, a sewer treatment plant, and some land. The estate was $4,000,000 in debt with 60% vacancy. I was able to turn that around within a three-year period and put it in the black. We increased to 100% occupancy, which was terrific, but I realized we still were not going to be profitable in our market. Long story short, I ended up buying the corporation from my family. I hired a contractor and realized the contractor was taking advantage, so I fired him, found a partner and started my own construction company knowing nothing about construction.

Within three years, we held all of our licenses and had 36 employees. We were exploding with business! This was prior to 2005, and I saw the market bubble coming, but I did not think that it was going to happen to me. Boy, was I wrong! Funding froze everywhere. We did everything we could to stay afloat, and I had to eventually tell 36 families that I could no longer employ them. That was devastating to me. It took me three years, but I paid everybody to whom I owed money and returned to California. By 2010, I had lost $20 million of my own money. Believe it or not, I called this my 'blessing.' Understand, I was working 18 hours a day, 7 days a week. My health was suffering; I had no freedom; I had no life! In a sense, I was trading time for money, even though I was the boss. When my 'blessing' happened to me, while devastating at the time, it was the best thing that could have happened to me. It shaped me as an investor and as a person. It taught me about money and how to treat it. It taught me about my risk tolerances. It taught me that I had integrity and strength I never knew I had.

After stepping away from real estate for a short time to regroup, I came back into investing, and I was terrified. But I networked, started wholesaling, fixing and flipping as well as investing in tax liens and tax deeds—all the while regaining my confidence. I have done just about everything there is to do in real estate investing. When I found Notes, 'angels sang' for me! It fit everything I was looking for: less risk, higher returns, chunks of cash and monthly cash flow, and CONTROL! I control the outcome, and I'm not speculating or dependent on any market, or person, for that outcome. It's a perfect form of investing for me, and for those who seek higher returns with less risk.

Can you share a lesson you learned early on as an investor that makes you a more valuable real estate investor today to work with?

Paige Panzarello: I have skinned my knees—like I said, successful people are successful because they have failed and learned from it. I know EXACTLY what my risk tolerances are—I am risk-averse. I like to invest based on fact and numbers, not speculation. I had people believe in me before 2008 that I owed money when the crash happened, and I was going to do everything in my power to not let them down. I paid every one of them. When I have investors' money, I take it very seriously. I know what it is like to lose, and I choose to be very conservative in my investments because of that.

What's the most important question women should ask themselves as they consider where they are today, where they want to be tomorrow, and how they plan to get there?

Paige Panzarello: If you ever listened to a real estate guru, they'll ask you, "What is your 'why'?" I like to challenge people with "What is your 'what'?" What I mean by that is, what is it that you need right now (chunks of cash or monthly cash flow)? And that changes as you grow as an investor, but what is it that you need right now to get to the next level? Once you determine what that is, put a number to it. You also have to be realistic regarding your immediate goals. And then you pick a vehicle to get you to that next step, and then once you get to that next step, go back to redefine what is your 'what' and use a vehicle to get you to that next step. That will get you where you want to go.

What would you say are three qualities that a woman who is reading your chapter should consider when choosing a real estate investor to work with?

Paige Panzarello: Number one is trust. If you don't have 100% trust in the person you're partnering with, you should not invest with them. Period. Don't be distracted by flash and promises of huge returns. This is your hard-earned money. It is your job to protect it. The second thing is the alignment of goals and realistic outcomes. If the person that you're seeking to invest with is promising you the world, it's likely not realistic. The third thing is integrity. Really dig deep. Are they telling you what you want to hear, or do they actually have your best interests at heart? Is it about the money for them, or is it about the relationship? Are they really going to do everything in their power to protect you and your money, even over themselves?

For a woman who might say, "I'm already earning six figures" or "This sounds good, but I don't have the bandwidth to add anything else to my plate," why should she still consider adding real estate investing to her portfolio?

Paige Panzarello: Life happens every single day. You might be earning six figures right now, but what happens if that company goes belly up? What's your backup plan? How much have you saved? You might be in a great position now, but that doesn't guarantee that you're going to be in a great position later on. Real estate investing can also be passive. You can have a very full plate, but if you can find somebody that you're comfortable with and let them do the heavy lifting, you can benefit.

It's my passion to prepare people so that when life does happen to them—and it will, if it hasn't already—they're going to be ready and not broken.

How can someone find out more about you and your real estate opportunities?

Paige Panzarello: Go to CashflowChick.com and book a free consultation with me, or they can sign up for my email newsletter. BuildingWealthwithNotes.com is the workshop that I teach, and you will learn everything that I do to invest in Notes and protect your invested dollars, or you can learn how to do it yourself. Or, go to TheTryllionGroup.com.

About Paige Panzarello

Company: The Tryllion Group and Cashflow Chick

Who I can help: Anyone seeking to build wealth outside of the stock market in a safer investment and make their hard-earned dollars work for them so they can spend time enjoying life with family and friends. And they can sleep well knowing their financial future is secure and intact.

What sets me apart: I am a real estate investor with over 20 years of experience in all forms of real estate, with a specialty in distressed mortgages (non-performing notes) multi-family properties, and self-storage.

Testimonial:

"Paige (the Cashflow Chick) is a joy to work with. My wife and I invested with a Self-Directed IRA in a note with her over two years ago. Payments are always received on time (and sometimes early!). We recently decided to renew our agreement for another year and have decided to invest with her on a performing note with non-IRA funds. I really like not having to worry as much about tenants and toilets. Thanks, Paige!" –Shawn F. in Stafford, VA

How to get in touch with me:
Email: Info@CashflowChick.com
Website: CashflowChick.com or BuildingWealthwithNotes.com or TheTryllionGroup.com

Social Media:
Facebook, Twitter, LinkedIn: Paige Panzarello or CashflowChick

Scan here to learn more:

Getting Your Start in Real Estate

Are you a woman who has always dreamed of pursuing real estate investment but aren't sure where to start or who to work with? Carolyn 'CJ' Matthews, a co-founder of National Platinum Group, is here to show you the ropes with practical, invaluable advice on how to get your foot in the door by investing pragmatically and wisely to benefit yourself and your family.

As an experienced business coach specializing in residential assisted living, Carolyn understands the ins and outs of real estate investment and the myriad ways it can transform and benefit the lives and careers of women of all ages, offering financial security and stability that can last a lifetime.

With care, honesty, and understanding, Carolyn will show you how to start your own business and build wealth that will put you in a position to pass down to generations and leave a legacy that your children's children can benefit from. There's no time like the present to get started on taking hold of your future.

Conversation with Carolyn 'CJ' Matthews

Thank you so much for joining us today. Can you share your full name and the company you represent?

Carolyn 'CJ' Matthews: I represent National Platinum Group.

Carolyn, tell us about your company and why investing in residential assisted living homes can change and positively impact a woman's life.

Carolyn 'CJ' Matthews: When you invest in real estate and find a good investment that's steady and allows you to get good returns at the same time, even with the up and down cycles of real estate, you want to jump on board. That's basically what we offer at National Platinum Group. Medical care is a growing industry and super important, and we're creating ways in which that's very beneficial to our society and creating cash flow for our investors.

What types of investment opportunities do you offer and how much is required for an initial investment?

Carolyn 'CJ' Matthews: Our specialty is syndicating, so people can join in, and that can be a debt or an equity investment. If it's debt, we would borrow the money from a group, and they would get anywhere from 8 to 12 percent return on that money per year. Simple interest only, and then in three to five years, they would get their initial investment back. If it's an equity investment, many times people will purchase the home and have us run the business in the home. And what that allows them to do is own a piece of real estate with a very steady tenant with a long-term lease that can pay them over the normal going rate for a single family home.

We do project management, we work in partnership with you, and we also create our own deals. If we're doing a certain type of PPM or a grouping of money, usually our minimum investment is about $50,000. However, we do have people who group up with lesser dollars to create a $50,000 or $100,000 or $200,000 nest egg that will loan us the money, and then we return it back to the treasure chest. So, that means you wouldn't necessarily need to be an accredited investor. It's a great way to get started in real estate investing.

What kind of return on investment (ROI) do your projects offer, and typically how long does it take to recoup an investment?

Carolyn 'CJ' Matthews: Three to five years. There are three ways in which we purchase or create the business. One is, we purchase the real estate and the business that is already up and running. The second way is, we purchase the real estate, rehab it to fit the needs required for assisted living and then put the business in it. The third way is, we build from scratch—dirt to door. All those ways work for investors, depending on their portfolio and tax strategies. Within three to five years of the original purchase, we refi out. That could be a refi with a commercial loan, could be an SBA loan; it could be a variety of things like that. And then their initial investment goes back to them, depending on what the deal is; sometimes if they are an equity partner, then they would get a percentage of the cash flow of the deal along with their payment.

Why is investing in real estate advantageous to women?

Carolyn 'CJ' Matthews: As Oprah says, "They're not making any more land." There's no more land really being made, and everyone always needs a roof over their head or a place to do their business. Everyone's always going to be dealing in real estate, either buying, selling, renting, or leasing. And if you know what you're doing, you can actually make good money. It can be a job, or it could be a passive investment or an additional income stream for you while you work your regular job. The stock market feels a little manipulated. Your returns in the stock market are a long-term play. And that's great for a lot of people, but as women, we're working our regular jobs, usually with family responsibility or raising kids solo, and there's only so many hours in the day. As a passive investor, that's even better for many people because you don't have to do any of the work, but you get the benefits. It's like having a great person working for you. Real estate is not going anywhere; it will always be here in some form.

What do you feel are the biggest myths when it comes to investing in real estate (and your asset class)?

Carolyn 'CJ' Matthews: The biggest one is, "If I don't have the money, I can't invest." I am a perfect example of that. When I first started in real estate, I was a single parent getting paid a minimal wage with a bachelor's degree! I had no money and no savings, yet I was able to purchase 14 houses in six months using other people's money (OPM). So, you can absolutely do it. You can get a lot of other people together and find a really good investment, vet the deal, and be a passive investor. You're finding the good team, you're researching the good team, you're looking at the numbers, you're checking out the niche, and then you take the treasure chest in, and you go invest the treasure chest, and that gets you into the business. You can get paid for that. It's a form of syndication.

What are some common misconceptions around the real estate industry, especially since the 2008 market crash, that are not true today? And why is now a good time to invest in real estate?

Carolyn 'CJ' Matthews: Anytime is a good time if you know what you're doing. Or if you are just starting out, you can research passive investing or turnkey investing. Just verify, do research, and yes, it's a little scary in the beginning. There are a lot of us women out there really willing to guide you through the process and help you take your first jump into the pool. The biggest misconception is that if the next crash comes, nobody has any money, and therefore, there won't be any money to be made in real estate. It's exactly the opposite. Whether the real estate is up or down, if you're buying right, and you plan appropriately, you're going to make money with your home or your commercial endeavor or whatever type of real estate you're looking at. And especially assisted living homes—because they have the protection of a steady business in the home that doesn't get affected by market downturns.

What are some of the most common fears you have found that women have about getting started in real estate investing?

Carolyn 'CJ' Matthews: Losing money. What I usually say to that is, make sure to manage your risk and loss. If you don't have money, find money to work with using the OPM method and find a passive deal or do the labor and have people invest in you. There is always a risk; however, you can mitigate that risk. Part of that is good money management; the other part is vetting the deal. If you don't know anything about real estate, passive investing with a treasure chest is a good way to start.

I'm here to tell you that there are ways to get into the real estate market. Again, I did not start with my own money. I was struggling. But I was dedicated and knew that I could do it. I was going to get it done, no matter what.

How can real estate investing make life better?

Carolyn 'CJ' Matthews: The biggest way is protection against job loss, downsizing, and age discrimination. I'm older now, and I see it in my friends. They've gotten older, and companies can go find somebody else that they can pay less. We also know that sexual discrimination still occurs. Unfortunately, I grew up with that, and we as women just worked around it, and real estate was one of the ways you could do that. Frankly, there is no sexism in real estate. Real estate is the great leveler. You want to buy a house, and you got the money, they'll sell it to you just as they'll sell it to somebody else. So, it does make life better because you have protection against job losses, it's an additional income cash flow for yourself, and it falls into retirement strategies and tax advantages really well. From a tax perspective, just having your business, which might be one rental home, is amazing for your taxes, especially if you're working an eight-to-five job. So, cash flow, retirement strategies, your taxes, and most of all, protection against job and income loss.

So, Carolyn, it sounds like real estate investing (in residential assisted living homes) is something more women should consider as a revenue stream and a way to stop trading time for money. I'm sure you've piqued some interest in what you've shared, but someone may be concerned as to where to find the money to invest in your projects if they don't believe they have access to capital.

How can you help a woman who is interested in real estate investing achieve the greatest success?

Carolyn 'CJ' Matthews: A big part of any success is your mind. Just because you don't know, it doesn't mean you can't figure it out. If you're concerned about not having the money, there is another way to create that—and that's other people's money. Let's say you don't know anybody, but you do know how to analyze a deal to see if it is worthy. Being able to communicate that with other people has a huge value

What really inspired you to go into real estate investing?

Carolyn 'CJ' Matthews: Real estate investing is a little bit of an addiction. I cannot go down the street without wondering how much that house will go for. But I'll tell you what really inspired me to do this. I used to be in long-term care insurance, and I also was raised with my grandparents. And they each had large families, so I was considered to be the youngest child of this aging group, and I saw